738.382 B977g   FV
BUSCHOR
GREEK VASE-PAINTING

30.00

Greek
Vase-Painting

Ernst Buschor

PLATE I.
THESEUS, ATHENA AND AMPHITRITE: KYLIX WITH THE
SIGNATURE OF THE POTTER EUPHRONIOS.

From Furtwängler-Reichhold, Griechische Vasenmalerei.

Greek Vase-Painting

Hacker Art Books   New York, 1978

TRANSLATED BY G. C. RICHARDS

First published, New York.
Reissued 1978 by
Hacker Art Books, New York.

Library of Congress Catalogue Card Number 77-73882
ISBN 0-87817-217-3

Printed in the United States of America.

CONTENTS

			Page
Preface			vii
Chapter	I.	The Stone and Bronze Ages	1
,,	II.	The Geometric Style	18
,,	III.	The Seventh Century	29
,,	IV.	The Black-Figured Style	63
,,	V.	The Red-Figured Style in the Archaic Period	111
,,	VI.	The Style of Polygnotos and Pheidias	133
,,	VII.	Late Offshoots	155
Index of Illustrations			161
Index of Names			174

PREFACE

A HISTORY of Greek vase-painting has been for a long time a desideratum of students of Greek art and antiquity. Many years ago I planned such a work, but the difficulty of the necessary illustration caused the plan to break down. In the meantime an extensive literature has grown up on the subject, mainly in German, but with contributions from other countries. In his first chapter Dr. Buschor has shewn how the result of excavation in Greece and Italy has been to throw our starting-point further and further back, until it lies in the Neolithic age. But it is not only in regard to the earlier phases of Greek vase-painting that research has brought light : the red-figured vase-painting which is one of the most perfect fruits of Greek art in the fifth century has been far more minutely and intensively studied. The result has been to fix the outlines, and more than the outlines, of the history of a fourth great branch of Greek artistic activity ; the history of architecture, of sculpture and of coinage having been already thoroughly investigated. And this fourth branch is not merely vase-painting ; but since the fresco and other paintings of the great age of Greece have almost entirely perished, we mav fairly say that it includes almost all that we can ever know of the history of early Greek painting. Vase-paintings can but feebly image the colouring of the great painters of Greece ; but they can give us invaluable information as to the principles of grouping and perspective adopted by them ; they can reflect the extreme beauty of their figure-drawing ; and they can shew us how they treated subjects from the vast repertory of Greek mythology and poetry

PREFACE

Most of those who take up the study of Greek art are strongly attracted by vases, the subjects of which are more varied, and the treatment freer than is the case with sculpture. For mythology, religion, athletics, daily life, they are first-hand authorities. Yet one may fairly say that, until a few years ago, satisfactory study of them was impossible. Vase-paintings, in consequence of the shape of the vessels themselves, can very seldom be adequately reproduced by photography. And the published drawings of them, until about 1880, were quite untrustworthy ; partly because the draughtsmen had insufficient sense of style, partly because most of the vases in the great museums were more or less restored, often in a most misleading way.

Thus merely to reproduce published engravings of the vases was quite misleading. The truth about them could only be known from a technical examination of the originals scattered through Europe. Yet one must say that in nearly all our English classical books and dictionaries, old engravings are uncritically reproduced. It is a fouling of the springs ; and however practically inevitable such a course may often have been, the result is that the reader never knows whether he is treading on firm ice or on a mere crust. Anything more reckless and misleading than the procedure of the publishers and editors of illustrated classical books can scarcely be imagined. The errors resulting can only be weeded out by slow degrees.

Since about 1880 things have slowly mended. The German Archæological Institute, and the French and English Societies for the promotion of Hellenic Studies have published really careful drawings of a multitude of vases, Mr. F. Anderson in England being one of the most accurate and careful of the artists employed. In the last few years the catalogues of vases in Berlin, Paris, Munich, London and other places have given authoritative informa-

PREFACE

tion as to restorations. A fresh era in the knowledge of technique and subject was begun by the magnificent publication of Furtwängler and Reichhold, with its splendid plates. At present the most authoritative works on early red-figured vases are those of an Oxford man, Mr. J. D. Beazley, and an American, Mr. J. C. Hoppin. Mr. Beazley has been good enough carefully to revise the present translation.

We have reached a stage at which, for all but specialists, what was most needed was a general history of Greek vases in all their periods, compiled by a trustworthy authority, and so fully illustrated (no easy matter) as to enable a reader to follow the text throughout. Thus would the whole subject be mapped out, and the approach to any particular province be made easy. Such a book is that of Dr. Buschor. His examples are carefully chosen; his text shews full mastery of the subject; and it is very unlikely that his treatment will be superseded for a long time to come. It is, however, a book not adapted for a mere cursory reading, but for careful consideration and study.

I may add a few words by way of introduction to the subject. We may divide the whole history of Greek pottery into two sections, which are separated one from the other by the line which divides primitive from mature Greece, about the middle of the sixth century.

Before that time, before the age of Crœsus and the rise of the Persian Empire, the history of Greece is very imperfectly known to us, through the traditions of the temples and the old families, which are seldom wholly to be trusted. Where history is uncertain it is of untold value to have monuments and works of human manufacture to supplement it. These provide a skeleton of fact with which to compare legend and tradition. It is now generally recognized that before writings in the form of inscriptions

and coins come into general use, pottery furnishes the most
continuous and most trustworthy material for the dating of
sites, indications of commercial intercourse, the movements
of peoples.   In recent years the study of prehistoric Greece
has made immense strides, primarily owing to the excavations of Schliemann, Evans and other investigators.   The
subject seems to fascinate the younger generation of
archæologists ; and the pottery found in the graves of the
early inhabitants of Greece and Asia Minor has been
worked at with great minuteness and to much result.   It
has revealed to us the outlines of the early history of Crete,
the Troad, Laconia, Thessaly, and a number of other districts.   Constant comparison with the results of finds in
Egypt which can be dated from inscriptions has revealed in
a measure the state of the civilization of the Ægean in
century beyond century, back to Neolithic times.

When Greek civilization became fully established, in the
sixth century, when inscriptions and coins begin to give us
far more exact information than that which can be derived
from pottery, the interest attaching to the latter does not
cease, but it changes in character.   We no longer go to it
to determine the outlines of the history of civilization.   But
it has now become a thing precious in itself because of its
beauty, its close relation to the poetry, the religion and the
life of Greece.   The elegant forms of Greek vases and the
charm of the designs painted on them have caused them to
be sought after by great museums and wealthy collectors.
The graves of Italy, Sicily, Hellas, have poured out a
constant supply of these works of art, some of them beyond
value.   Classical archæologists have naturally given much
attention to them ; and of late years the assignment of
examples to noted masters, and the study of their technique
have been zealously prosecuted.   They belong too wholly
to a civilization which has passed away to be readily under-

PREFACE

stood by ordinary visitors of museums ; but those who have once been bitten with their charm find in them an occupation, a delight and a solace which are great helps in life. Greece is the classical land of art in all its forms, and the principles of art which were established by the successive schools of art there can never be wholly neglected. If we set aside the pottery of China and Japan, which is, in another sphere, of unsurpassed beauty, the pottery of Greece is the only perfectly developed and thoroughly consistent pottery in the world ; and the noted productions of modern Europe seem in comparison poor and half-civilized.

Dr. Buschor's general plan has compelled him to write but in a summary way of the works of red-figured style, which are incomparably the most beautiful. In fact, in such small and rough illustrations as are possible in a handbook, their quality could not be reproduced. For them the reader must go on to other works, or visit the vase-rooms of museums. A conspectus of successive styles and periods was all that was possible. And I think that enough is here accomplished to arouse the interest of those who love art and have some sympathy with the Greek spirit.

The old supremacy of the Classics in education has passed away, and in future they will have to hold their own not by prescriptive right but in virtue of their intrinsic value, on which more and more stress is being laid by those who feel what their neglect in the modern world would mean. It is time to strengthen their hold by shewing how they lie at the very root of philosophy, literature and art. Our successors will not be satisfied with drilling boys in Greek and Latin grammar, but will have to insist on the place held by ancient peoples, the Jews, the Greeks and the Romans, in the evolution of all that is valuable and delightful in the modern world. We have to widen the field of Classics, and illustrate the literature from every point of view. And if

PREFACE

it be felt that the object of education is not merely to enable boys and girls to earn a living, but to help them to lead a worthy and happy life, then I have no fear that the Classics will be permanently eclipsed.

Mr. Richards' work as a translator was very difficult. In spite of kindred origin, the German mind in literary production moves on different lines from the English. Not only is the order of words in a sentence different, but the sentences themselves are much more involved, and German scientific writers aim at an exactness in the use of terms which we seldom attempt. Mr. Richards' version is very accurate; but it must be allowed to be not always easy reading. He preferred to retain as much as possible of the meaning, even if it involved some stiffness in the text. Students will thank him for this; and if the general reader finds that he has to give the text a closer attention than he is used to give to books, he will in fact have his reward.

Dr. Buschor's work is a solid stone for the temple of knowledge, and the main lines of the subject are now so firmly fixed by induction, that they are not likely to suffer very much change in the future.

P. GARDNER.

CHAPTER I.

THE STONE AND BRONZE AGES

STUDENTS of the history of Greek vases have been gradually led backwards from a late period to earlier and earlier stages of civilization by the course of circumstances. First of all graves were opened in Lower Italy; the first great collection of vases, formed by Sir William Hamilton, British ambassador in Naples, and published in 1791-1803, contained chiefly the output of later Italian manufactories. Next, from 1828 onwards, the doors of Etruscan graves were unlocked, and their contents proved to be the rich treasures of Greek red and black-figured vases, procured in such numbers by the Etruscans of the 6th and 5th centuries. About twenty years later a bright light was thrown on eastern Greek pottery of the 7th century by the discovery of a cemetery in Rhodes. About 1870 the 'Geometric' style became known and the Dipylon vases at Athens were revealed. In the seventies and eighties Schliemann's spade unearthed the Mycenean civilization, and in the beginning of the present century we were introduced to the culmination of this period in Crete. Finally in quite recent times finds of vases of the Stone Age in Crete and in North Greece have given us a view of vase-production in the third millennium B.C. If therefore we wish to retrace this long road, we must begin at a period, of which the investigation has only just begun and which presents most difficult problems.

The excavations in Northern Greece, *i.e.*, in North

1

Boeotia, Phocis and above all Thessaly, have introduced us to a purely *Neolithic* civilization. Here alongside of the two simpler prehistoric techniques, unornamented (monochrome) and incised ware, was discovered, even in the oldest strata, a richly developed painted style, with linear ornaments painted either in red on vases with a white slip or in white on vases made red by firing. The monochrome, red or black vases are often brilliantly polished and of excellent workmanship. In the later layers of the Stone Age finds this civilization differs considerably according to locality. One class of painted (and incised) vases is very prominent : it was found chiefly at Dimini and Sesklo, and shows quite a new principle of decoration (Fig. 1). It combines curvilinear patterns, especially the spiral motive, with rectilinear decoration (zig-zag, step pattern, chequers, primitive maeander, etc.) ; the colouring varies, white on red, black on white, brown on yellow. Side by side with this style we find in other places the greatest variety of painted and unpainted vases : even polychrome decoration appears. In the early Bronze Age all this splendour vanishes and gives place to the production of coarse unpainted ware.

It appears that this Stone-Age Ceramic of North Greece has no connection with the finds of South Greece, and is rather to be traced to the North and the civilization of the Danube valley.

The South presents us with a much more primitive picture. The large layer of Stone Age finds, which came to light in Crete, produced vases with incised geometrical ornament, alongside of coarse undecorated pottery, but curvilinear patterns of Thessalian type are completely absent and painted vases are rare. The reason for a less elaborate development of Neolithic civilization in Crete seems to be that it gave place to the Bronze Age compara-

2

tively early : in Thessaly it seems to go down far into the second millennium.

According to these early vase finds one has thus to picture to oneself the beginnings of ceramic art. First, the most essential household vessels are fashioned by hand out of imperfectly cleansed clay, and burnt black in the open fire, and before long the outer surface is also polished, probably with smooth stones. Rectilinear ornaments are pressed or incised into the soft clay, and by degrees the method of filling and indicating the incised lines by a white substance is learned ; the clay is also treated plastically, for instance channelled. Gradually the clay is made less impure, is more cleanly polished and more evenly baked in the oven, and by the actual firing has various colours, red, black, grey, yellow and brown, imparted to it. Thus a ground is also obtained for painting, on which the rectilinear ornaments are imposed with colour. Greater solidity and brighter colouring are obtained by covering the vase with a slip, which moreover sets off the painting excellently. The invention of the wrongly styled ' varnish,' a black colour glaze which, though technically undeveloped, appears even in North Greece of the Stone Age, is of the highest importance for the whole history of Greek vase-painting. The forms are primitive, little articulated, but already very various : the decoration covers uniformly almost the whole vase.

But the different techniques do not regularly succeed each other ; inventions are not immediately communicated from one locality to another ; primitive methods subsist alongside of more advanced, nay even sometimes drive them out again. This much is clear, that a section taken through these contemporaneous prehistoric civilizations would present a highly variegated aspect.

The Stone Age is succeeded by the Bronze Age, here

3

earlier and there later; here more quickly, there more slowly; i.e., metals are gradually introduced, and with them new techniques and a new civilization. It is evident that to the earlier Bronze Age belong a series of innovations which are of decisive importance for the history of vases, the invention of the potter's wheel, the perfection of the so-called ' varnish,' and the imitation of metal forms in clay. In most places the potter's oven and the painting of vases appear only in the early Bronze Age.

Into the early Bronze Age fall the finds from the earliest layers at Troy. In the unalterable faith that he was discovering the world of Homer, with the strong and weak points of a dilettante, Heinrich Schliemann began to dig at Hissarlik, and in the excavations of 1871, 1878, 1890 and 1893 Dörpfeld and he investigated the rubbish hill, which has become so famous, the nine superimposed settlements of which represent as many successive civilizations down to Roman times. The numerous ceramic finds of the five lowest layers show the transition from rude hand-made and ill-baked ware with impressed linear patterns to ever more developed stages. The potter's wheel and oven finally succeed in producing brilliant red, black, grey, brown vases of the finest technique. The variety of shapes is very great, some are already quite developed; the imitation of metal forms is to be traced here and there. A notable speciality is found in the so-called Face-urns (Fig. 2), rude imitations of the human form, produced by adding eyes, nose, mouth, ears, nipples and navel; and there are also other vase-types, which are not repeated in Western Greece. Painting is rare, the vases are either monochrome or adorned with incised linear ornaments, which are often applied in the manner of necklaces, or divide the vase vertically.

The Bronze Age civilization of the second city up to the fifth, which, judging by the rich finds of metal utensils and gold ornaments, was by no means primitive, recurs in the whole of N.W. Asia Minor and in Cyprus. Its last phase cannot be separated in time from the western civilization of the shaft graves (p. 7).

Parallel with Troy II-V and the mainland civilization of Marina (below), on the islands of the Aegean is the so-called Cycladic civilization. Its pottery, however, presents a much more variegated picture : beside the primitive vases there are vases incised and painted with rich, not exclusively rectilinear, ornamentation : glazed (' varnished ') vases also occur. The forms are very varied : bronze and stone vessels often serve as models ; the structure of the vases and the distribution of the ornamentation show unmistakeably definite artistic intention. There is great difference between various islands and a comprehensive view of the development is not yet possible. Specimens like the beaked jug from Syros (Fig. 3) are probably contemporary with the early Minoan style of Crete (p. 7), but the pans with engraved spirals, circles, ships and fish are later. On Melos, which has quite a separate position of its own, the influence of the Cretan ' Kamares ' civilization (p. 8) in technique and decoration is obvious.

We return to the mainland and Central Greece. Hagia Marina in Phocis is the chief place in which a pottery, following on the Neolithic, has been found, hand-made with a black or red glaze, with or without rectilinear ornaments in white. This was called ' Primitive varnish ware,' before the Neolithic preceding stages had become known. 'Marina' ware superseded the Neolithic in Boeotia (Orchomenos) and Thessaly also ; similar vases have been found in the western islands (Leukas) and in the Argolid (Tiryns). It is also related to the Cycladic civilization, as is indicated by the jug imitated from metal models, which is common to both styles.

5

The ' Marina ' layer is succeeded at Orchomenos by a ware of a totally different kind, which probably spread from this locality and is therefore called ' Minyan,' dark-grey and grey or yellow vases, especially (*a*) drinking-cups, with tall channelled foot, and (*b*) profiled two-handled cups (Fig. 6), turned on the wheel, and in shape more plainly even than the Marina ware dependent on metal models. The wide extension of this already finely developed ware combines a series of bronze-age sites into a chronological unit, the so-called ' Shaft grave ' stage (p. 7). In Northern and Central Greece as well as in Leucas it follows on the ' Marina ' ware, in Attica and Aegina it takes the place of the monochrome and incised ware, in the islands it supersedes the Cycladic pottery, in Troy it is parallel with the ware of Asia Minor and Cyprus, in the Argolid the Marina finds of Tiryns are followed by the shaft graves of Mycenae with Minyan vases.

Almost everywhere along with the Minyan ware we find vases not so finely constructed, generally hand-made, which are neither burnt dark nor glazed, but show a decoration applied in dull colour. This lustreless painting (*Mattmalerei*) in Central and Northern Greece, and also in Attica (white-ground ware of Aphidna, Eleusis), uses only geometrical ornaments; in the Argolid on red or light clay vases linear patterns, wavy lines, running spirals or even figured decorations (*e.g.* birds, Fig. 4) are painted in brown colour. The decoration generally emphasises the shoulder; the lower part of the vase is unadorned and separated by stripes from the upper.

The next stage is that Minyan ware and lustreless painting are almost everywhere driven out by Creto-Mycenean ' Varnish ' pottery. In many places this process did not take place till the end of the Bronze Age, as in Thessaly, Central Greece and Attica (Eleusis). It was apparently the lords of the Argolid who first and most freely opened their gates to Cretan importation and influence; in the shaft graves of Mycenae, famous for their rich treasure of gold, discovered by Schliemann in 1874 behind the Lion Gate, the oldest Cretan import in the shape of vases of the first late Minoan style (p. 10), appears beside Minyan and lustreless ware (Figs. 4 and 6).

By the side of these local products, the ' Varnish ' vases in the shaft graves appear like children of a strange and sunnier world, representative of a quite different and superior style of art. The idea that they came from Crete has been confirmed by the excavations carried on since 1900, which in different parts of the island disclosed a compact civilization of markedly un-Greek character, developing without a break from the third millennium to the end of the second, which is in striking contrast to that of the mainland. This civilization has been named Minoan after the fabulous king Minos, the builder of the labyrinth, and it has been divided into three epochs, of which the first two precede the period of the shaft graves.

In the early Minoan period, following on the miserable Stone Age (p. 2) the Cretans must have laid the foundation of their riches, if an inference may be drawn from the stone vases and goldsmith's work of Mochlos. The ceramic art enters on two paths, which have a future before them. The vases were hitherto unpainted and only incised. Now *either* they are covered with brilliant black paint ('varnish') on which the old patterns are painted in tenacious white colour, a technique which celebrated its triumph in the subsequent period, *or* the vases are left in the colour of the clay and painted with bands of ' varnish '; to this so-called ' Mycenean ' technique belongs the whole late period (p. 10). There is a special group of flamed ware, the patterns of which, like much that is Minoan, are far nearer

7

to modern applied art than to Greek. Even in the first half of this period the kiln seems already to be known; the potter's wheel appears in the second, which is characterized by the first appearance of curvilinear patterns, especially the wave series and running spiral.

The Middle Minoan period, a pure and richly-developed bronze civilization, is the height of polychromy: the clay is finely cleansed, the black glaze is at its very best, red in different shades occurs besides white. A transition leads to the brilliant period of the Kamares style, named after the first discoveries in the Kamares cave on Mt. Ida. The ' Mycenean technique ' occurs not infrequently alongside of the polychrome; but as it often edges the ornaments with incised lines or puts white spots on them, it does not reject the tendency to richer effect, which is a feature of the age and is also expressed in the relief-like ornamentation of many vases. (Barbotine). The ornamentation is still very fond of linear patterns, and also develops the spiral still further, and lays the foundation of the numerous decorative motives which characterize the later periods; living creatures also (birds, fishes, quadrupeds) are represented in painting. The motive of drops falling from the brush, which would be inconceivable in Greek vase-painting proper, occurs already. There is a simultaneous use of decoration in bands, and without division; the emphasizing of the shoulder by ornamentation is found in contrast with the lower part decorated, if at all, with stripes (Figs. 3 and 4). The stock of forms increases, and the imitation of metal-work is often unmistakeable.

In the Kamares style proper (Figs. 5 and 9) polychromy (white, red, and dark yellow on black) reaches its highest development, the greatest variety of plastic decoration appears, the Mycenean technique (dark on light) is relegated to the background.

The shapes become continually more delicate, metal vases are often directly copied; cups, beaked jugs, beaked saucers, and amphorae with handles at the mouth are specially common. The list of ornaments is much increased and can scarcely be described in few words. By the side or in the place of geometrical motives, crosses, zig-zags, groups of strokes, and richly developed circle, bow and spiral motives, appear vegetable, leaves, branches, rosettes, and most important of all, the continuous wavy tendril. Even living beings appear occasionally.

The plant ornamentation of the Kamares vases is in a peculiar relation to nature. Though nature is here for the first time consistently imitated, the reproduction is not at all 'naturalistic' but thoroughly and from the first severely stylized. Not only does the colouring bear no relation to the object represented, not only is the combination of vegetable and geometric motives of purely decorative character, but the natural object imitated is often barely recognizable. The Kamares potter only aims at a pretty combination of colour and line, not at representations. Nor is he concerned with structural arrangement: division by bands and emphasizing the lower part of the vase by leaves pointing upward are uncommon. Usually the decoration spreads freely over the field and is not subordinated to the structure of the vessel. This undisputed predominance of the ornamentation is in the sharpest contrast to the procedure of Greek art proper.

The Kamares civilization, starting from Crete, exercised influence over the islands of the Aegean: the importation and imitation of its ware can be proved for Thera and Melos. Isolated finds in Egypt are of importance, first because they prove the relation of Crete to the Nile valley, and secondly because they give a fixed date (XII Dynasty). The technique did not disappear with the Middle Minoan

Age, but was long maintained alongside of the new style.

The Kamares finds come mostly from the older palaces of Phaistos and Knossos. The investigation of their ruins has shown that these buildings were destroyed by fire and soon afterwards replaced by still finer new edifices. The vase finds in these later palaces show a complete break with the old style. Polychromy is no longer the principal attraction ; it is given only a secondary place : the new style (Middle Minoan III and Late Minoan I, Figs. 7, 8, 10 and 11), which is no longer satisfied with gay ornamentation, but with fresh vigour essays the conquest of Nature and her excellences, throws off the bands of the old technique, and with bold freedom depicts the newly discovered world in dark colour on light clay. In contrast to the Kamares style, it did not arise on the vases themselves by the enrichment of an ornamental style, but it is to be understood as the reflection of higher techniques. Vase-painting gives only a small extract from the rich array of subjects, which the other lesser arts and the wall-painting of the period conjure before our eyes. Of the wonderfully vivid representations of men and animals, in which the Cretans were masters, nothing is to be found on the vases. This is certainly not an accident, but a sign of the purely decorative feeling of these artists. They did not want to stylize the human or animal body till it became decorative, to distort it for the eye by placing it on a curved surface, and by combining figures to upset the ease and flow of the decorative scheme. Thus they entirely gave up all reproduction of them, and are thus in marked contrast with Greek vase-painting, the history of which may be regarded as a constant struggle to represent mankind and animal creation. The Cretans took to other objects instead, which could be represented in the vigorous way they aimed at, and yet also filled the field decoratively, without any loss to the picture from the curve of the vessel. The vegetable world had entered the decoration of vases in the Kamares period : now it does so afresh, but in a totally different spirit. Grasses, branches, ivy, crocuses, lilies as they grow and wave in nature, surround the vases. But these people were specially concerned with the sea, marine plants and live creatures. Lotus flowers, sea-weeds and reeds wave in the water, the cuttle-fish stretches out his feelers, the nautilus swims about, starfish and snails, corals and sea-anemones surround the living objects, and dolphins gambol around.

What impelled the Cretan vase-painters thus un-weariedly to represent the marine world exclusively on vases? The explanation can only be sought in that supreme law of the development of artistic style, the talent for invention in a few pioneer brains and the slowness in invention of the many. The excellent idea of having the cool liquid in the vases surrounded by this decorative play of marine life, which filled the field and was so life-like, perhaps came from a single gifted brain. The idea became popular, and the common run of vase-painters created countless variations of the theme.

The excellent naturalism directly inspired by nature, which it transfers with a bold brush to the vases, is limited to a short creative period : immediately the schematic and conventional assert themselves ; life disappears, but fixed decorative formulæ remain, and to them the future belongs. Moreover, the stylized ornamentation never ceased to exist alongside of the natural ; nay, often appears on the same vase in conjunction with it, in the shape of wavy lines, spirals in different combinations, continuous tendrils (which are also treated naturally) or stylized plants. Thus two methods of decoration are in contrast, one ' tectonic ' with arrangement in bands, another, which freely scatters naturalistic representations over the vase, a kind of ornament which

11

has made almost everyone who has spoken of it adduce the parallel of Japanese art. The freely adorned vases are also most characteristic of the art of the Cretans, and show most plainly their gay and heedless manner, their free decorative work, their direct relation to nature, foreign to abstraction and idea : they set this art in contrast with the contemporary old civilizations of the Nile and Euphrates as well as with the Greek.

The naturalism of the first Late Minoan period has narrower limits than has been usually estimated. Not only is the stock of themes scanty (Fig. 11 is an exception) ; but also the reproduction of nature is purely superficial, knows nothing of perspective or shading, and stylizes the forms into the style of decorative drawing : thus, for instance, the marine world is represented without any indication of water. Of course, this does not mean that such abstraction from reality is not an advantage from the point of view of decorative art. Often the vase-shapes show a cultivated feeling for form in the way the body swells and contracts, but appear simple and constrained when compared with the fine lines of contour in the next period. Among new types that emerge may be mentioned the ' stirrup vase ' (Fig. 10) and the ' funnel vase ' (Figs. 7 and 8).

The superiority of these Cretan vases to all contemporary ceramic output showed itself in a vigorous export. The Egyptian finds of this ware give as a date the XVIII dynasty, approximately 1500 B.C., a date confirmed by some Egyptian objects found in Crete. Cretan vases were also exported in quantities to Melos and Thera : there the native industry loses itself in imperfect imitations of this imported ware. The Cretan civilization also enters the Greek mainland, especially the Argolid. The shaft graves of Mycenae (p. 7), from which the Late Minoan civilization transplanted to the mainland has been named ' Myce-

12

nean,' are the oldest instance of this fact. The imported vases of the six graves are distributed over the whole of the first Late Minoan (early Mycenean) period, containing late specimens of Kamares style and early specimens of the Palace style : but the bulk of the ' varnish ' vases found on the mainland belong to the succeeding period.

The second Late Minoan period of vase production in Crete, the so-called Palace style (Figs. 12 and 13) is not so sharply divided from the first, as the latter is from the Kamares style. Both phases are connected by several transitional forms and run parallel for a time. An important difference is that the last traces of the Kamares technique (the imposition of white, red and orange on a black ground) disappear : there is simply painting in black on light clay (Mycenean technique). The decoration neglects the neck and foot of the vessel and emphasizes the shoulder, particularly with the characteristic half-branches. The animated reproductions of nature in the preceding style are treated in a fanciful way ; they become fixed and are changed into ornaments and patterns for filling ; the significant unity of the design is interrupted by foreign elements ; the marine and plant ornamentation now never covers the whole vase but retires into a single band. In short, the naturalistic style gives place to a tectonic style, the representations are not the chief thing aimed at, which is the filling of the space. Beside the ornaments produced by the schematizing of living natural forms come new ones, which often look like a borrowing of architectural forms ; moreover, the juxtaposition and combination of the ornaments show the same spirit, and also the emphasis now laid on the shape of the vase, in which the structure and the swinging contour reach their highest form of elegance, as can be seen most plainly in the amphorae.

This art had a wide influence outside Crete. To the

13

beginning of the period, the transition from the first to the second Late Minoan style, belong many mainland finds, especially from domed tombs, in Peloponnese (Vaphio, Argos, Mycenae, Old Pylos), in Attica (Athens, Thorikos, Spata), in Boeotia (Thebes, Orchomenos) and in Thessaly (Volo). The finds continue during the period of the developed Palace style. The majority of these 'varnish' vases seem not to have been imported from Crete but made by Cretan artizans in the country. The Mycenean local princes, who from their lofty citadels controlled the surrounding country, surrounded themselves more and more with the splendour of this southern civilization, ordered weapons, ornaments, precious vases from Crete, used them in life, gave them to the dead in graves ; they also took into their service foreign artists, and gave employment to Cretan masons, painters and potters.

The islands too acquire Cretan vases : they were exported as far as Aegina, Melos, distant Cyprus, and the sixth city of Troy.

About the end of the second Late Minoan period the Cretan palaces of Phaistos, Knossos, and Hagia Triada are destroyed, and with the destruction of these and other sites the Palace style decays.

The pottery of the Late Mycenean (or third Late Minoan) period (Figs. 14-17) is very inferior to that of the Palace style. The technique is at first neat but afterwards falls off : the smooth yellowish clay takes a green tinge, the brilliant glaze colour, often burnt red, becomes a lustreless black. The ornamentation consists of the last remains of the naturalistic decoration, now become quite lifeless and poor, with which are associated purely geometrical patterns of the simplest kind, wavy lines, spirals, concentric circles. Rectilinear patterns (groups of strokes, hatched triangles) become ever more prominent. The decoration is generally very loose, emphasizes the shoulder band, and usually puts on the lower half of the vase only a few stripes : vertical division of the field into ' metopes ' is common.

But, on the other hand, figured representations are not unusual on late Mycenean vases. Two classes can be distinguished off-hand : —(a) animal representations, in traditional ornamental style and very ' geometrical ' in treatment, particularly birds with cross-hatched bodies, certainly continuations of the old lustreless painting (cp. Fig. 4 with Fig. 15) ; and (b) larger compositions taken over from wall-painting, often provided with ornaments to fill the field, like the chariot-race on the krater from Rhodes (Fig. 17). The best-known example is the Warrior vase from Mycenae representing the departure for the battle-field.

Apart from these figured representations, one may say that Cretan vase-painting, after its brilliant achievements in the Kamares, shaft grave, and Palace styles, sinks down to that primitive level from which it started : it becomes once more a geometrical style.

The area over which we find this pottery is enormous, being practically the whole Mediterranean basin, Crete, Egypt, the Cyclades, the coast of Asia Minor (sixth city of Troy) and its adjacent islands (e.g. Rhodes), Cyprus (where the Mycenean supersedes an old and plentiful pottery akin to that of Troy), Phoenicia, Italy, Sicily, and especially all important sites of the Greek mainland. In many places, where the ' varnish ' painting did not enter earlier, it now comes into contact with the old indigenous technique, with the monochrome, incised and lustreless vases : many backward settlements, like Olympia, seem to have had practically no acquaintance with the Mycenean style.

Here again the Egyptian finds give us a date : they last from about the end of the 15th down into the 12th century.

But since it is not conceivable that we should date the Geometrical period, which followed the Mycenean, back into the second millennium, the late Mycenean style must have lasted at least four centuries; the rate of development, which in the time of great achievements had been very rapid, must have become considerably slower.

To arrange the huge mass of late Mycenean vases in this long development is impossible, until the material has been sifted and worked through. But one thing already can be said with certainty, that it was not merely exported from Crete; indeed it is more than questionable, whether Crete played the leading part. In this period the native seat of the brilliant Minoan civilization is no longer in the foreground; the centre of gravity has shifted to the mainland, in particular the Argolid. Even in the period of the shaft graves we see the Peloponnesians eagerly adopting Cretan civilization; in the following period the mainland vies with Crete in the production of Mycenean vases, and finally must have wrested the lead from the southern outpost. This applies not merely to civilization but to political conditions. A hypothesis, in favour of which there is much to be said, connects the destruction of the Cretan palaces with the invasion of conquering 'Achaeans,' the name Homer applies to the lords of the mainland. Just as the wall-painting originally borrowed from Crete was still flourishing on the mainland, when it had died out at home, so the late Mycenean pottery must have been produced mainly in continental Greece, and the new style must have been formed by the Peloponnesians. Thus we can explain the non-Minoan elements, the strong geometrical influence on the decoration, and the taking over of figured scenes from wall-painting, which was rejected by the old Cretans.

So it was probably the 'Achaeans' who spread the late Mycenean pottery all over the Mediterranean. They had

16

become a seafaring nation on a great scale. Of their entry into Crete we have just spoken, of their united campaigns of conquest in Asia Minor, in which the Cretan king has the Argive Agamemnon as his overlord, the Homeric poems tell us, and of their colonizing expansion in the Mediterranean the vase finds among other things give evidence, as they justify conclusions about new localities of manufacture (Troy, Rhodes, Cyprus, etc.).

In the beginning of the first millennium the scene is totally altered. On the coast of Asia Minor and the islands are settled Hellenic races, among which the Aeolians and Ionians are probably descendants of the emigrated Achaeans, while the Dorians represent a new tribe come in from the north, which subdued the Peloponnese and Crete and extended to the south of the Aegean Sea.

These shiftings of population, the so-called Dorian invasion, with which Greek historians begin the history of their country, mark the end of the Bronze Age and of the Mycenean civilization. Iron weapons, only sporadically to be found in the late Mycenean age, take the place of bronze; the Mycenean vase style vanishes all along the line, and gives way to a new style, the Geometric.

CHAPTER II.

THE GEOMETRIC STYLE

NOW for the first time the history of Greek vases proper begins. In the pottery of the geometric style are latent the forces, which we see afterwards expanding in contact with the East, as well as the oldest beginnings that we can trace of that brilliant continuous development, which led to the proud heights of Klitias, Euphronios, Meidias. Its producers may be unreservedly described as Greeks : Hellas has come into being. However primitive the civilization of this early Greece may have been, however patriarchal is the picture which Homer, the great genius of this period, gives us of this world, however much the works of art described by him point to Mycenean reminiscences and Phoenician importation, yet in the department of ceramics the art of this time was thoroughly original and highly developed, and it is from the vases that this early phase gets its name.

We should like to have a glimpse of the origin of the Geometric style, but its beginnings are shrouded in darkness. It cannot be regarded as simply a descendant of the pre-Mycenean Geometric pottery, which in outlying parts continued throughout the Bronze Age ; for in its ' varnish ' technique, its forms and decoration, it is totally different from those primitive vessels. As little is it a direct continuation of the Mycenean style, from which it took over the technique of painting. However much towards the end of its development the latter inclined to decoration in

18

bands and the geometrizing of ornament, it was an outworn poor style that arose out of schematizing of living forms, in complete contrast with the clear concise Geometric style, which consistently unfolds and exhausts its individuality.

Naturally the Mycenean style did not disappear abruptly from the face of the earth, and there are transitional forms, which cannot be nicely divided. They must not be too highly estimated; they are, it is true, at the beginning of the new development, but do not influence it. Thus the ' Salamis ' vases, and their parallels from Athens, Nauplia, and Assarlik in Southern Asia Minor, show this transition, retaining in part Mycenean forms like the stirrup vase, and Mycenean ornaments like the spiral, but being in fact an insignificant ware, of bad workmanship and meagre decoration. More interesting is the survival of Mycenean traditions in Crete, the home of the Minoan style, and in the Argolid, the chief seat of late Mycenean civilization : certain vase-shapes, hatched triangles, concentric circles and semi-circles on the shoulder are retained from the old style.

From these and other Mycenean reminiscences the unfolding of the new style cannot be explained any more than by a revival of pre-Mycenean Geometric styles. We must rather bring in, to explain the phenomenon, those movements of peoples, the driving out of southern Mycenean civilization by races advancing from the North, and the new mixture of blood, which strengthened and made dominant the northern European element. Though the Dorians did not develop the style as conspicuously as other tribes, there arose out of the ferment caused by their appearance on the scene the new creative vigour, the Greek element proper, which, out of the frozen traditions of the mainland and the lifeless relics of Mycenean art created a new style and a firm basis for a fine development.

19

The Geometric style makes a virtue of the necessities of rude beginnings; out of the simple decorative material at its disposal, it creates a rich system. Angular patterns, rows of dots, strokes, ' fish-bones,' zig-zags, crosses, stars, hooked crosses, triangles, rhombi, hook maeanders, maeanders broken up in different ways, maeander systems, chequers, net patterns are most common; alongside of them are circles and rosettes neatly made with the compass. The wavy line, which like the snake edged with dots perhaps comes from Mycenean polyps, takes a second place; all other free ornamentation is eschewed; the place of continuous spirals is taken by circles connected by tangents. Thus the ornamentation appears to be steeped in mathematics, and the same is the case with the representation of living beings. Man and animal alike appear in stylized silhouettes, which bring the various parts of the body into the simplest possible scheme, and set them off sharply against one another. Thus the human breast appears as an inverted triangle and is shown frontally, but the legs and head are in profile. The head, which is only emancipated from the silhouette style in the succeeding period, already often has a space reserved in it to indicate the eye. As a rule the human body is represented naked, while towards the end of the period, the instances of clothing, especially of women, become more numerous. There has been division of opinion as to whether this nudity reproduces actual life. That is certainly not the case. " This is the nudity of the primitive artist, of the abstract linear style. It is not man as he actually is, but the concept ' man ' which is to be rendered, and clothes are no part of this concept." (Furtwängler). These oldest Greek representations of man are not, properly speaking, reproductions of nature, but a kind of mathematical formulæ, which gradually in the course of centuries of fresh observation of nature become richer, corporeal, living, spiritual. Animal representation begins also in the same formulistic manner. The choice is in contrast with the Minoan animal world : there is complete absence of the Oriental animal world of fancy ; we only see the Northern fauna ; horses, roes, goats, storks, geese. The animals stand upright, graze, or rest with neck turned round. The technique is always that of the pure silhouette ; only the birds often, as in the pre-Mycenean and late Mycenean styles (Figs. 4 and 15), show hatched or cross-hatched inner drawing of the body.

These geometric ornaments and abstract silhouettes of men and animals form the complete stock out of which the artist of the period provides for the decoration of his vases. With them he fills the bands into which he loves to divide the vase (Fgi. 18) ; or at all events the shoulder or handle band, constructively the most important, in which case he covers the lower part of the vase with black (Fig. 19) or with parallel rings (Fig. 23). The bands, the breadth of which is varied, are filled in two ways. Either we have continuous ornaments, and processions of animals, chorus dancers, warriors, chariots and horses, which in this style are essentially nothing but ornament ; or he divides the bands, and particularly the handle bands (Fig. 19) vertically into rectangular fields, metopes as they are called. The metope naturally takes a different scheme of filling the space from the band ; if the latter prefers a continuous series, the former requires ornaments complete in themselves, like circles and rosettes, or in the case of figures, the antithetical group, the heraldic opposition of two different fields of figures, or of two figures in the same field. The figures connected by compulsion of space are then more closely united by a central motive, and there arise ornamental compositions not at all drawn from actual life, *e.g.* two birds both holding in their beaks a fish or a snake, two

21

horses with crossed fore-legs, rearing towards each other, tied to a tripod, or held by a man with a bridle, two roes with raised fore-legs leaning against a tree. Band and metope with their compulsory schematism no longer suffice for the growing need of representation : in the large vases the chief band is often made very high, or in the upper part of the vase a rectangle adorned with ornament or figures is left out from the surrounding black : thus arises the vase with special field for subjects.

Legend, which in this period found its brilliant expression in the Epics of Homer and Hesiod, is still very much in the background in these vase-paintings. Centaurs only begin to be represented on late Geometric vases. Scenes such as the embarkation on the bowl from Thebes (Fig. 21) cannot be interpreted otherwise than mythically, as the rape of Helen by Paris or of Ariadne by Theseus, since on Geometric bronze fibulæ from Boeotia it is certain that legendary scenes are intended. The battle scenes too, with their duellists surrounded by spectators and their fights on a large scale by land and sea, must be inspired by the Heroic Saga. But far more numerous are the scenes of daily life, which are connected with the sepulchral purpose of the vases. We see the dead man lying on the bed of state, covered with a big cloth ; men, women, and children, with arms raised to their heads in token of grief, are standing, sitting and kneeling around him ; we see the bier placed on the hearse, and amid loud lamentation of the populace driven to the cemetery, while, in honour of the deceased, chariot-races and mimic battles are represented and dances are performed to the sound of flutes and lyres.

As the human form is rendered without any feeling for bodily shape, so all the representations are without any spatial sense. Chariot floors and table surfaces are not fore-shortened, the breast of the dead man lying on the bier

22

is represented in front view, the covering of the corpse is visible in its complete extent, as if it hung down upon it ; in the case of pairs of horses the off horse is simply moved forward and represented smaller ; masses of men are rendered by files of similar figures ; figures to be thought of as in the background, *e.g.* the hinder rows in the Helen bowl (Fig. 21) are placed high up. The space, which contains the figures, is an ideal tectonic space, the surface of the vase to be adorned. Where the figures do not suffice to fill this space, the Geometric artist regards it as a gap in the decoration of the vase and fills the void with dots, rows of zig-zags, hooked crosses, rosettes with a central point, and actually paints birds or fishes between the legs of horses or between the chariot and the bier which rests upon it (Fig. 20).

This even covering of the surface gives the vases of this period a carpet-like appearance, and this textile impression is strengthened by the geometry of the ornamentation, by the angular stylization of the living beings, by the decorative schemes and the division into bands. But on this account to derive the whole style from the imitation of works of the loom would be a mistake ; the stylistic limitations of the style cannot be identified straight off with the technical limitation of weaving. As in all primitive civilizations so in the formation of the Geometric vase style, simple linear patterns may have been taken over from weaving and plaiting : but this is not the case with circles and rosettes, and anyhow such a consistent and systematic perfection as that of the Geometric vase style is inconceivable as an imitation of a foreign technique.

Greek ceramic art never completely lost this 'textile' character, and never quite renounced the Geometric school through which it passed, though by centuries of labour it freed itself from the defects and crudities of that

23

school. Vase-figures long exhibit their origin out of the ornamental silhouette ; the decorative schemes of arrangement in rows and of antithetic groups are always breaking out afresh ; the principle of using up the space is applied superficially for some time and only gradually refined ; the decoration in bands subsists for a long time beside the vases with a pictorial field, and remains of it exist till late ; the disinclination for deepening the field, based on a correct structural feeling, goes through the whole history of Greek vases and keeps the ornamental figure world of the vases always at a distance from the much less constrained world of free painting.

The Geometric vases have not merely a historical meaning, but a value of their own. They are not a preliminary stage, but something complete. In them Greek art in true Greek fashion worked out a thought ; expressed itself for the first time in a classical way, if the phrase may be used ; out of a clumsy rustic style with poor ornamentation developed vases of technical perfection, compact and clear in form, consistently thought out in the decoration now lavishly, now sparingly spread over them, in their austere beauty true children of the Greek genius.

But this style did not put out everywhere equally fine flowers. It was not, like the late Mycenean, an 'imperial' style, but, from the first—and this is significant for Greek art—differentiated and conditioned by locality ; each region had its own manufacture of vases, and its own Geometric style. Already the lead is taken by that place, which later was to drive out of the field all competitors, viz., Athens. The Dipylon vases—the name usually given to Attic Geometric vases from the fact that most of them were found in the cemetery before the Dipylon Gate,—rise in form, technique and decoration to the greatest perfection and highest richness. In the magnificent amphoræ, as much as two metres in height, which are worthy of their monumental use as tomb decoration, the Geometric style perhaps reaches its culmination; in the so-called black Dipylon vases, often only sparingly decorated on the shoulder or neck and otherwise covered black, we get already an effect of colour which became popular much later; the stock of forms is ampler, the maeander more developed, the delight in telling a story and in representing a scene greater than in other Geometric styles. Beside the Dipylon there is a second site in Attica, Eleusis, though not so important; Boeotia too must be mentioned, the pottery of which makes a provincial impression, and is dependent in forms, patterns and subjects on Attica and the Aegean islands, as also that of the neighbouring Eretria in Euboea.

The prototypes of the big Boeotian and Eretrian amphoræ with high stem and broad neck have been found particularly in Delos and Rheneia, richly ornamented vases ' de luxe,' in which the painting is laid on a white slip. In the same place, where the cult of Apollo had a great attraction, several other Geometric classes were also found, among them the precursors of the art which flourished in the 7th century and which is usually ascribed to the island of Melos. On the Delian vases horses and human representations occur, but generally in this class there is a disinclination to represent figures. The same disinclination and the frequent use of a light slip characterize the pottery of the Dorian island of Thera, which developed a very definite though sober and monotonous Geometric style that seems to have obstinately persisted till well into the 7th century. The rich finds of other classes bear witness to an active trade with the mainland, other Cyclades, and the Ionic East, the pottery of which has many points of contact with the Cycladic. We know it from Miletus and other places on the Asiatic coast, but above all from the island of

Rhodes. The Rhodian Geometric vases are distinguished from the Cycladic by the absence of the light slip, and seem in spite of many points of contact never to have reached the same level. An isolated vegetable ornament, the so-called palm-tree, points to relations with Cyprus. Cross-hatched rhombi and birds are very much in vogue; they appear also in loose arrangement on the ' Bird kylikes,' which in post-Geometric times extended from Rhodes over the Ionian region and so made their way to the Greek mainland, Italy and Sicily.

The most important Peloponnesian manufactures are : (1) that of Sparta, which now to some extent adopts the white slip later predominant; (2) that of Argos, which soon discards its Mycenean reminiscences and develops on parallel lines with the Attic ware without attaining to the heights and richness of the Dipylon vases ; (3) above all, the so-called Protocorinthian.

This Geometric style, which next to the Attic had the greatest future before it, seems to be at home in the Northern Argolid (p. 34). Its early Geometric beginnings we do not know. It is akin to its Argive neighbour in many points, in the scantiness of its stock of forms, in shapes like the metallic krater with a stirrup-handle. Unfortunately little has been left to us of the large-sized vases, kraters, cauldrons, amphoræ and jugs. The two-handled cup (Fig. 23), the round box, the globular oil-flask, the deep drinking-cup, the jug with flat bottom (Fig. 33) are the favourite smaller shapes. The limitation of the decoration to the upper margin, and the decoration of the rest with parallel stripes is characteristic. This ware was more exported than any other Geometric class; it entered the southern Argolid, went by way of Corinth and Eleusis to Boeotia and Delphi, and was exported to Aegina and Thera, Italy and Sicily. On Italian soil, in the Euboean colony of Kyme, it certainly founded a branch factory, which quickly took on a local character and exported in its turn ; but in various other places also the style evoked local imitations.

The Protocorinthian style owed its brilliant future both to the Geometric foundation, and, as will appear, to the strong influence of Cretan Art. In Crete, after the settlement of the Dorians in the island, no definite Geometric style was formed : the Mycenean traditions were too strong and the relations with the East too close. After the purely Geometric vases, among which wide-bellied amphoræ without a neck are common, there soon appear vases showing Cyprian influence, particularly small jugs with concentric circles on the body (precursors of Fig. 27) ; thus a pitcher from Kavusi, which by an exception has figures on it (a charioteer and mourning women in a metope-like arrangement) is apparently, in shape as well as in the ornament which consists of a row of ' S's ' on their backs and the un-Geometric drawing of its silhouettes, dependent on similar Cyprian models.

Crete with its loosely-rooted Geometric style took up the new elements more freely than other localities, where at first they are placed side by side with the native ones, like the palm-tree on Rhodian vases, the Cyprian circles on Attic and Protocorinthian jugs, the precursors of the tongue pattern on Attic and Theran vases, the unsystematic rays on Attic and Protocorinthian ware, the running spiral probably borrowed from metal work on Protocorinthian and Theran vases. Moreover, figured representations from an alien world of ideas creep into the fixed Geometric systems, as for instance the two lions devouring a man on a Dipylon vase, the goddess flanked by two animals on a Boeotian amphora, the fabulous creatures on Rhodian vases.

These foreign elements, which have their root in

27

Oriental art, are the harbingers of a complete revolution, and in them is heralded the end of the Geometric style. It is obvious that a decorative style like the Geometric could have no future : its possibilities were quickly exhausted, even where the style was most richly developed. Its dissolution would have come, even if superior civilization with richer methods of decoration had not been in close contact of trade and intercourse with this early Greek world, and exercised on it a persistent influence. The Cretans and Eastern Greeks lived in the immediate neighbourhood of Egypt and Asia, the islands and the mainland were united to the East by active trade relations. In particular Phoenician merchants, while the Geometric style was flourishing, handed on to the Greeks the products of Oriental art, as both the Epic and the finds testify. Nor did the Greeks remain at home either, but had long become a seafaring people; Attic, Boeotian and Protocorinthian painters proudly place representations of ships on Geometric vases ; the statistics of the finds of the various Geometric wares show a constantly growing trade intercourse. Colonisation too has already begun, and is ever expanding ; according to the earliest vase finds Syracuse, Kyme, and perhaps also Massilia and the Black Sea coast received settlers, while their mother-cities still had Geometric pottery. Since Syracuse was founded in the second half of the 8th century and its oldest graves contain late Geometric vases, we obtain an approximate date for the end of the Geometric style.

The objects of Oriental Art, which were brought before the eyes of the Greeks by this active intercourse, powerfully stimulated their fancy. The crowd of decorative motives from vegetation, the world of fantastic animals, and the superiority of Oriental Art in the rendering of life, drew Greek vase-painting out of Geometric uniformity and pointed it to new paths.

CHAPTER III.

THE SEVENTH CENTURY

AS the Oriental motives pour into the Greek world, a new development begins, which in the details of its course is still hard to grasp, the collision of the native Geometric style with Oriental influence, the fusion of both elements into a new unity, and the growth of the archaic style. In contrast with the quiet and consistent unfolding of Geometric style, the process to anyone who goes deep into its details takes on the character of a restless fermentation, and an almost dramatic tension. It occupies, roughly speaking, the 7th century. Without forgetting how arbitrary divisions in the history of Art must always be, let us here treat as one the period from the end of the Geometric style to the abandonment of filling ornament, the change in technique of clay and colouring, and the formation of the established body of black-figured types.

The smelting process took on a different character in the different regions, according to the tenacity with which the old style was retained, and the intensity of the contact with the East. In most places there follows first a period of hesitation and experimentalism, out of which finally the new style is formed. Nowhere does the Oriental element simply take the place of the Greek Geometric; the acquisitions of the old style, the fixed vase shapes, the principles of decoration, and the technique, remain and are further developed. Greek pottery was much too highly and richly developed, too, firmly rooted, to find it necessary to imitate Oriental clay vases. The stimuli were of much more general nature; they are chiefly visible in the ornamentation and pictorial types, they are taken from metal vases and richly embroidered materials, from costly carpets, articles of jewellery, engraved gems, and other fine things, which the foreign trader or the seafaring Greek brought from the Near or Far East or saw with his own eyes abroad. It became apparent to him, that the Geometric style was really poverty-stricken and mathematical. The feeling for finely-drawn line and vivid reproduction of life awoke in view of the freer Art of the East; the Greek made the Oriental models his own and created out of them and the mathematical element a new Art. Not all stimuli come direct from the East; perhaps only comparatively few, which were then passed on, were constantly altered and took on varied local colour. It looks as if the stream of Oriental influence took two different routes, one by way of the Greek East (Rhodes, Samos, Miletus) and another by way of Crete, which evidently had a strong influence on the Cyclades and Peloponnesus.

In Crete Phoenician metal objects have been found, which were imported during the Geometric period, and the Cretan Geometric pottery soon takes up motives of decoration borrowed from the Oriental or Orientalizing metal industry. The row of 'S's,' which plays a part in Geometric bronzes, appears as we have seen on the Kavusi jug (p. 27). Its climax is the cable pattern (*guilloche*), which is obviously borrowed from Phoenician metal vessels (Fig. 26). The tongue pattern (Figs. 25-27) which surrounds the lower part and the shoulder of the vases, like the rays similarly used (Figs. 31-35), goes back ultimately to Egyptian plant calyces. The connection with bronze patterns is fully proved by the dots often placed on the ornaments, by the technique of adding white on black painted vases (Fig. 29)

30

which aims at a metallic effect, and by the change of the vase shapes. These often get a quite non-ceramic appearance (Fig. 25), and in their rounding and contouring, especially by the emphasis on the foot (Figs. 25 and 27), they are in contrast with the Geometric forms. The Praisos jug (Fig. 26) is obviously under Cypriot influence, as is the delicate Berlin jug (Fig. 27), in which a previously described class (p. 27) reaches its high water mark. The Praisos pitcher (Fig. 25) to the Orientalizing patterns enumerated already adds the hook spirals, which are characteristic of the 7th century, and the Berlin jug adds also the volute and the palmette. The plastic head which crowns this little bottle, and is entirely inspired by the Egypto-Phoenician ideas of form, inaugurates a new era in the representation of man. We are now in the time when Greek sculpture was born, in that notable period when Greek art under the influence of Oriental art took to the chisel, to enter on a century of development which ended in giving shape to the loftiest and most delicate creations that can move the spirit of man. It is noteworthy that Greek tradition embodied the beginnings of this development in a Cretan, Daedalus, and to a kinsman of this ancestor of all Greek sculptors it traced back the invention of the great art of painting, without the influence of which we cannot conceive of vase-paintings henceforward.

The first period of the transitional style betrays little of this influence. The reproduction of living beings is dominated by the decorative figures of the East, especially monsters and fabulous beings, which now make their entry into Greek art, and exercise a powerful attraction not only on plastic art, but on poetic and mythopœic fancy. Thus the Geometric silhouette is superseded. If even the preceding age had felt the need of leaving void a hole to indicate the eye, now the head is completely rendered by

31

an outline and made lifelike by interior drawing (Fig. 30). The next stage is that the whole body also is rendered in contour. To make the transition plain, we show here a vase-fragment, the Cretan origin of which is not established, but which must be in close connection with Cretan art, the Ram jug from Aegina (Fig. 28). The animal frieze, with its hook spirals, dot rosettes, rhombi and triangles to fill the space, is characteristic of older Oriental art; the drawing of the rams is far beyond Geometric technique; in the body too the silhouette is given up, and indication of the hide is attempted. This animal frieze is no longer an end in itself: by the men clinging to them the ornamental rams become mythical rams, the rams of the Odyssey. The fugitives are not very closely connected with their saviours, and the giant must have been more than blind not to notice them. But on the other hand the artist has drawn them very clearly, has put both arms and both legs in view of the spectator, and even, where a small detail would not other-wise have shown well, made a small nick in the belly of the ram. This shows how the artist of the period could with difficulty do without a clear outline.

These attempts are perfected in the outlined figure of a plate from Praisos, which is certainly Cretan (Fig. 29). The childishly disproportioned structure has now become a clear organism of genuine Greek stamp, full of excellent observation of nature; the ornamentally constrained picture becomes now a free version of a legend, which however cannot be interpreted with certainty, till the white object under the sea-monster has been explained. It is most likely that we may see in it the foot of a female figure filling the left half of the plate, perhaps Thetis, who escapes from the attacks of Peleus by changing into a fish. The interior incised lines in the body of the sea-monster are a novelty, which the ceramic art has developed indepen-

32

dently (p. 37). But on the other hand the advance in drawing and the technical rendering of form, the outline of Peleus, the light colour of the woman, the reddish brown tint of the rider on the reverse, cannot be explained apart from the influence of free painting, whose oldest stages are stated to have been outlining with progressive drawing of interior details, monochromy (i.e. outline drawing with a filling of colour) and distinction of sex by colour. After an interval of several centuries wall-painting must have sprung up again and flourished in Crete, different to be sure in essentials from the Minoan, rather influenced by the East like the decorative art of the time. In spite of the tendency to represent painting as 'invented' in Greece, Greek tradition reluctantly admits that this art was indigenous and highly developed in Egypt long before.

The bloom of Cretan art seems not to have outlasted the 7th century. Finds give out, and tradition expressly testifies to the migration of Cretan sculptors to the Argolid, a district which also took over the inheritance of Cretan vase painting.

Of the two chief centres of Argive Geometric vase fabrication, one which is to be sought in the region of Argos and Tiryns cannot be followed out very clearly. The oldest Greek vase signed by an artist, the krater of the potter Aristonothos with the blinding of Polyphemus (Fig. 30), seems from the shape of the vase to belong to this class. The complicated shape of the circle of rays, the breaking up of the head silhouette, the juxtaposition of the traditional sea-fight with the legendary scene, are typical of the early Orientalizing period; certain parallels with the late Mycenean Warrior vase (p. 15) perhaps justify the conclusion, that remains of the old wall-painting had an influence on the style. Like the Aristonothos vase, some stirrup-handled kraters with metope decorations continue Argive

Geometric traditions. These vases, however, are exclusively found in the West (Syracuse) and were probably made there; they do not give faithful reflection of their Argive prototypes. A krater with tall foot and ornamentation in bands, found at the Argive Heraion, representing the rescue of Deianeira, with plentiful use of 'monochromy,' is too isolated to make a picture of this Orientalizing pottery possible.

It cannot have played a leading part, but must soon have been put in the shade by its near neighbour and rival. For that the so-called Protocorinthian fabrication is also at home in the Argolid is proved by the fact that the chief places, where the ware is found, are Argos and Aegina, and that quantities of small and hardly exportable ware are found at various places in the district. The alphabet of the inscriptions agrees with this locality, and so does the style, which leads up to the Corinthian, whence the name has been given, as well as the fact that the great trading-centre of Corinth looked after the sale of the wares; for the area in which they were sold is identical with that of the Corinthian vases. On account of these close relations with Corinth, the home of the Protocorinthian vases has been sought with great probability in the neighbouring town of Sicyon, of which we are told that it was the place to which Cretan artists migrated, that it was the birthplace of Greek painting and seat of a flourishing metal industry, so that we are able to account for three ingredients of the new style. For the Protocorinthian style of the 7th century gave the most delicate development of Cretan 'Daedalic' types, particularly near its end; fixed a clear style of figure representation and an ample store of types, and developed its vase-shapes, system of decoration and technique, under the influence of metal patterns, more severely, precisely and richly than any other contemporary centre of fabrication. In it the vase history of the post-Geometric century culminates.

Even in the Geometric period which preceded it (p. 26) (the sparing ornamentation of which is in contrast with the Dipylon pottery and its greater delight in using the brush) metallic influence can be traced; the simple running spiral certainly comes from incised bronzes. The delicate two-handled cups closely connected with the Geometric style (Fig. 23), with their well-cleansed clay, improved glaze colour baked black to red, and the reduction of the walls almost to the thinness of paper, can only have been produced in competition with the metal industry; and as a matter of fact delicate silver vases of the same shape have been found along with the clay copies of them in Etruscan graves. The lower part of the cups is at first painted black, but soon it is surrounded with the circle of rays, which according to the ideas of the new period emphasizes and makes clear the tectonic character of that part of the vase. This motive also appears in the Geometric decoration of the flat-bottomed jugs (Fig. 33), the unguent pots which show Cyprian influence in their oldest globular shape, the kylikes, round boxes and other shapes, though not always in the typical place, and often also combined with other ornaments (Figs. 30 and 32). In spite of its Geometrical treatment and its truly Greek close combination with the system of decoration, it does not disown the impulse it owes to Oriental patterns (p. 30). The Protocorinthian style also introduced its doubling (Fig. 32), which still survives in the 6th century (Fig. 98). The cable pattern, borrowed as has been shown from Oriental metal-work, drives out the 'S's' and the running spiral. As a handle ornament it gets a rich enlargement (Fig. 32), the fine stylization of which, no doubt, was first produced in metal industry. Of the greatest import-

35

ance is the adoption of loops, volutes, running tendrils and friezes of arcs, which in combination with the palmette appear on the wall of the vase or as an upper stripe, and from simple, often loosely stylized beginnings, expand with the help of the lotus-flower into a fine loop and flower ornament ('Rankengeschling'), as in Figs. 31, 32, 35. That this ornamentation, in spite of its rigid stylization, was felt by the Greeks to belong to the living vegetable world, is shown *e.g.* by the volute-complex, behind which the hunter (on the lowest stripe of Fig. 31) waits to catch the hare, as well as behind the naturally drawn bush (on Fig. 36); this shows that the 'volute tree' (Fig. 34) flanked by two sphinxes, is thought of as a real tree. On the other hand the ornaments in the field are quite as meaningless as in the older style: to those used by Geometric artists are now added the hook spiral, and the rosette treated as a dotted star, two ornaments we have seen already on the Ram jug (Fig. 28); at first they are independent and can be used to form friezes, later they become less and less prominent (Figs. 32 and 34, cp. also Fig. 28). Two further decorative motives lead us back into the region of metal-work, the scale-pattern extending over the whole body of the vase (Fig. 38), which so often occurs in incised metal-work, and the tongue ornament, the typical decoration of bronze vessels, which on clay vases as well often rises over the foot in place of the kindred rays, but most commonly finishes the shoulder where it meets the neck. Both motives have already been met with in Crete, as applied on a black ground. The black ground technique of the Praisos jug (Fig. 26) is very popular with Protocorinthian artists, goes alongside of the clay-ground vases for the whole period, and supplies richly coloured examples decorated with figures and ornaments of fine effect, particularly in combination with a new technique, which appears in the advanced style, being specially typical of scale and tongue ornamentation, that of incision. It is perhaps idle to inquire into its invention : it is more important to establish the fact, that it was first consistently and systematically applied to the black-ground vessels of the Protocorinthian artists, who were also famed for metal-work, and gave a new stamp to the style at a time when the East used simple brush technique almost exclusively. The incised line is always combined with the addition of coloured and particularly red details.

The technical advance, which in some measure replaced the influence of the rising art of painting by that of metal-working, is shown more plainly in the figured representations, particularly the friezes of animals, which the vase-painters, inspired by Oriental metal ware and embroideries, with ever greater zest employ on their vases. Beside the birds, stags and roes, beside the dogs pursuing hares, with which a lower stripe could be easily filled, come new animals, for which they are chiefly indebted to Oriental art, bull, goat, bear, ram, wild-goat, lion and panther, sphinx, siren, griffin, and other hybrids. These creatures appear in quite definite types, which admit of little variety : it is characteristic that the panther's head is drawn in front view, perhaps through an abbreviation of a heraldic double panther; and this rule is devoutly observed through the whole period of decoration with animal friezes. An indication of this is that the decorative animals never become pure outlines like the human figures, but after a period of partial silhouette (p. 31), return to the complete silhouette, as satisfying better the requirements of decoration. This return became possible through the use of the incised line, by the help of which interior drawing could be added on a black ground, and the effect of the figures was further enhanced by the addition of details in red. This is an important innovation in the history of Greek vase-painting.

GREEK VASE-PAINTING

The general effect of the vase is completely altered by the decorative play of colour, which extends also to the ornamentation, and takes on that gay many-coloured aspect which is so characteristic of the older archaic period, and which is only dropped late in the 6th century. The new colour system does not aim at realism ; it makes prominent for decorative purposes single parts of the animal body, especially the neck and belly.

The drawing of the human figure proceeds on other lines than that of animals. In consequence of the new development of the art of painting (p. 33), it makes a fresh start. First we have the vase of Aristonothos (Fig. 30) ; the next stage is represented by the Ram vase (Fig. 28) ; the desire of distinguishing the lighter skin of women from that of men leads to the tinting in brown of the male body. But in the formation of the figure types certainly it was not only painting that stood godmother, the metal worker's art must also have asserted its influence ; the kinship with Cretan and Argive flat bronze reliefs and metal engraved work is too great, the sharp clear-cut types too much in the spirit of bronze technique, for it to be possible to postulate an independent development. To this corresponds the fact that the outlines of the figures are accompanied by incised lines on polychrome vases with black ground, on the finest of the later lekythoi (oil-flasks) and on the Chigi jug (Fig. 35). This technique is repeated on the big two-handled cups with finely stylised figured representations, which finally accomplish an important advance already foreshadowed by small and hasty specimens : the dark silhouette with incised interior detail, prevalent in the style of the animal friezes, and along with it certain details like the circular rendering of the eye, are taken over for the representation of male figures.

This adoption, which only takes place at the end of the development, and makes the Protocorinthian style the

38

starting point of black-figured vase painting, does not unite heterogeneous elements. For man and decorative animal are equivalent in their juxtaposition, and beside the free mythological scenes there is a series of representations, which seems to have grown straight out of the animal frieze. The Centaur, the old Greek forest monster, joins the animals; winged demons in the remarkable scheme of running with bent knee (pointing to the metope treatment) are also placed amongst them; kneeling archers shoot arrows at them, hunters and combatants pursue them, Bellerophon rides on Pegasus against the Chimaera, Herakles fights against the Centaurs. Purely human scenes, like the favourite Duel (Fig. 43), are simply flanked by animals. The addition of figures in rows and overlapping makes this simple combat into a battle; wounded fall, corpses are hotly fought over, auxiliaries hurry up. The artist always in these cases gives prominence to the finely decorated shields, the pride of Argive metal industry. Like the rows of fighting men, the other frieze-like compositions, the processions of riders and chariot-races, the hunting scenes and chase of the hare, thanks to charming observation of detail, make a direct appeal which is strange for such early art. The bushes in the hare-hunt of the Chigi jug (Fig. 36) show the awakening of the landscape element, which to be sure is always a rarity on vases and must have played a larger part in free painting. Moreover, the varying colouring of the animals on the stripe in question, which appears also on a frieze of riders (Fig. 31) and continues in Corinthian painting, must come from the same source, whereas the bold front view of the Sphinx head (Fig. 37) like that of the panther head and the Corinthian quadriga, was attempted for the first time in an ornamental band. Hand in hand with the enlivening of the friezes goes the suppression of field ornamentation: it is only sparingly applied, limited to the animal friezes or entirely absent. At times a lizard (Fig. 34), a swan or a monkey comes into the figured scenes.

Of course this is all devoid of meaning; for in spite of all progress and freer treatment the style is merely concerned with the decoration of a surface; ' exigencies of space ' are its supreme law. These control the type of the human figure, for even where it is not essentially an ornamental scheme, like the runner with bent knee, it fills from top to bottom the stripe assigned to it, extends its breast frontally, and reaches out its arms, as if it were yearning for a frame. And as the body avoids all perspective, so the head in profile shows its most expressive part, the eye surmounted by the brow, in full extent, and renders the long hair falling down over the neck as smooth surface, and the curly forehead hair as spiral. There is no rendering of folds to show depth in the drapery, which now the artist in true Greek fashion treats in an abstract way, unlike reality. The human figure remains a type, a homogeneous constituent part of the stripes, which are entirely designed for filling space. It matters little, if between chariot-race and lion-hunt on the Chigi jug (Fig. 37) a double Sphinx is inserted as central motive, or Bellerophon lays the Chimaera low in presence of two Sphinxes (Fig. 34); if close to the lion-hunt in the same stripe, Hermes leads the three goddesses before the fair Trojan shepherd, and if the names of the personages are entered in the field with big letters as a kind of ornamentation by way of filling: the incipient delight in telling a story is taken at once into the service of filling the field.

As the human figure still appears almost completely on a par with the ornamental animal figure, so there is little trace of any superior weight being attached to the scenic representations in the decorative system. Where the painter employs them, it is true he puts at their disposal the chief frieze and often one at the base in addition, but he frames them with prominent stripes of ornament or animals, and side by side with the narrative vases purely decorative ones are still produced. The presence of several animal friezes on a single vase (*e.g.* on jugs of the shape of Fig. 35) is not uncommon ; like band ornamentation in general, it is in contrast with the practice of the Geometric period (p. 25) and is probably to be traced to a strong influence of Oriental textile art. For the most severely shaped black vases, which are nearest to the bronze models that we possess (Fig. 38), do not always adopt this fundamentally non-tectonic breaking up of the body of the vase.

The close connection of the shapes with metal-work has been already proved in the case of the cups of early Orientalizing style (Fig. 23), and goes through the whole history of the fabric, and even where the models were not immediately copied, gave the vase-shapes a clearness and precision, with which the products of no other manufactory can compete ; the Sicyonian-Corinthian school of repoussé work perhaps originated many metal vase-shapes, which were afterwards used in various manufactories. Though the Protocorinthian list of shapes is only known to a small extent, an important change can be established. Beside the jugs of primitive construction (cp. Fig. 33 with Fig. 54) appear later more rounded vessels, the jug with ' rotelle ' (Fig. 38) and the wineskin-shaped, the chief example of which (Fig. 35) with its excellently decorated bands, sometimes black, sometimes in the ground of the clay, shows us the style in a richer and more developed form than any other vase of this fabric. In the same way the little ' lekythoi ' which are technically often quite exquisite, change their appearance, exchange their old globular shape (Fig. 27) for a slimmer one with pronounced shoulder, which the caprice of the potter often furnishes with plastic additions, Argive transformations of Cretan ' Daedalic ' types (Figs. 27 and 31). And as beside the ' rotelle" jug, we have the wineskin-shaped jug, so beside this sort of 'lekythos' there is a wineskin-shaped variety with a rough tongue-pattern on the neck (Fig. 39).

The ' lekythoi ' were the chief exported article, or at least the most favoured grave-offering of the customers abroad. But one cannot call it the favourite shape of Protocorinthian workmanship : it must not be forgotten that we have only an accidental selection of this ware, due to the discovery of two native sanctuaries (the Argive Heraion and the Temple of Aphrodite in Aegina), and many graves in the Argolid, Attica, and Boeotia, in the East (Thera, Rhodes, Asia Minor) and in the West (Sicily, Italy, Carthage). Wherever this ware came it exercised a stimulating influence, and in many places evoked local copies (p. 52) ; more than other districts the West was dominated by this Art. As the oldest Etruscan wall-paintings, those of the *Grotta Campana* at Veii and the *Tomba dei Leoni* at Caere, are quite under the influence of Sicyonian-Corinthian painting, so the class called into existence a multitude of imitations in Sicily and Italy, particularly at Kyme.

The extraordinarily wide currency of the ware denotes not merely its superiority, but also that of the trade-centre which exported it. This need not necessarily have been identical with the place of manufacture. Many signs, especially the occurrence of the vases in quantity in the Corinthian colony of Syracuse, point to the fact that the great trading city of Corinth took over the sale of the ware and gradually replaced it by its own products. The vases localized with certainty in Corinth by their alphabet give an immediate continuation of the Protocorinthian, and one can only ask whether this manufacture simply transferred its chief workshops to Corinth or whether Corinth in the closest imitation of late Protocorinthian ware developed a new style, which thanks to the commercial capacity of the Corinthians could drive the older competitor out of the field : its sphere of influence, as we saw, replaces the Protocorinthian, nay, encroaches still further on the Ionian region (Samos, Naukratis, Pontus).

The Corinthian style did not long retain the metallic clearness and precision of its predecessor, neither in its shapes, which for the most part it takes over (Figs. 35, 38, 39, 43), nor in its decoration, which exhibits the final triumph of the ornamental style. The dark ground technique becomes rarer ; the scaly fields continue for a time, white rosettes painted on the black neck and edge are in favour to the end ; the indispensable tongue ornament on the shoulder gradually comes to be rendered by the brush. The animal-frieze vases, which are quite in the forefront of the interest, link on to the later Protocorinthian in decoration and in the style of the figures, but soon alter the types in the sense of a broader rendering of form, and the rosettes in the field also show this change. On the common ware, which was turned out along with the good, one gets as a result coarse animals and filling patterns like mere blots ; but even technically perfect vases show a strong inclination to overfill the field, which one might bring into causal connexion with the Corinthian textile art famed in antiquity, if the vase picture repudiated the brush technique more than it does.

The composition shows the same intrusion of a strongly decorative element. The heraldic scheme is more prominent than ever. We owe to it the invention of a new ornament, a combination of lotus-flower and palmettes (Fig. 39), which like the old volute-tree (Fig. 34) is flanked

43

by two animals. In particular the wineskin-shaped and globular unguent-pots (Figs. 39 and 40) (Alabastron and Aryballos), the successors of the Protocorinthian unguent-pots, are decorated with it; but even in the stripes, which have not got the ' palmette and lotus cross,' there are groups of three animals at a time inspired by the heraldic scheme (Fig. 41). The list of types grows: beside the quadrupeds appear many birds (*e.g.* geese, swans, eagles, cocks and owls,) fishes and serpents; a motley series of hybrids, bearded sphinxes, winged lions, winged panthers, tritons and other fabulous creatures are side by side with the favourite winged demons, sphinxes, sirens and griffins. The place of the central ornament is often taken by purely human beings, especially the runner with bent knee, and the goddess of beasts (πότνια θήρων) which in the Oriental patterns are flanked by animals; but also non-ornamental figures, women, riders, grotesque dancers (Figs. 40 and 43) are found in this place. Thus arises a co-ordination of man and decorative animal similar to that of Protocorinthian art; anyone who has followed on the vases this process, which is characteristic of the 7th century, is not surprised, when in the archaic Corinthian pediment at Corfu mythological scenes appear side by side with the Gorgon flanked by panthers, and when in the representation of the central animal the myth begins to be active.

The non-ornamental human figures in the animal compositions are of course not invented for this purpose, but borrowed from other contexts, scenes of human life, which existed beside the decorative representations and followed the lead of the Protocorinthian precursors. They are certainly more intimately connected with the animal figures. The male figure (p. 38) has finally discarded the old outline drawing with brown filling for the animal-frieze technique, black silhouette with incised interior details.

But at the same time the memory of monochromy is not yet quite extinct; the head silhouette is still by preference painted red. When often instead of it the breast and thigh are picked out in red, when in sphinx and siren contour drawing is abandoned, the connection with the animal-frieze style is complete, and the new intrusion of a strong decorative element in this pottery is obvious.

Even the compositions of the figured scenes are under this decorative spell, which, as in the Protocorinthian style, is only broken through by a few gifted masters. The duel flanked by sirens on the Boston cup (Fig. 43) is typical of the older Corinthian style. The warriors and riders are often arranged in processions, collected in big battle-scenes; the grotesque revellers and dancers with extended posterior, prototypes of the satyrs, fill whole friezes with their reckless antics; the girls take hands for the dance. Special legendary scenes are, however, very rare, and when vase-painters like Chares supply names to an ordinary series of riders, this makes clear rather than removes the defect.

This defect to be sure is due to a great extent to the accidental preservation of a series of vases, which are for the most part careless decorative work intended for the export trade, so that we may form erroneous ideas. The neighbourhood of Corinth itself has supplied some fine specimens with a marked character of their own, which bridge the gap between the Chigi vase and later Corinthian vase-painting (Figs. 64-67), e.g. kylikes where, in the interior field framed by tongue pattern ornament, are fine Gorgon masks and human busts, and especially two works signed by the painter Timonidas. The flask with the story of Troilos (Fig. 44) shares with the Chigi vase the contrast of colour important for Corinthian painting. The flesh of the women is light as a set-off to that of the men, the chiton of the man sets off his nude parts, the shield its bearer, the front horse the hinder of the pair. The delight in the land-scape element, the fine steeds, and big inscriptions, points back to Protocorinthian style. But nothing is left of the ornaments scattered about the field but a small palmette, the composition has become looser, there is much less tendency to cover the surface in the drawing of the figures : the old scheme of the kneeling runner has its echo in the Achilles lurking in ambush, but it is ingeniously adapted to new use. Thus there is a much freer relation to space, which gives the necessary foundation for the descriptive style. The hunter too, whose outline Timonidas has put on a clay votive tablet unconstrained by the silhouette tech-nique or by the desire for contrast of colour (Fig. 45), is not crowded by any filling ornaments ; the finely drawn youth in the balance of his proportions and the rendering of detail surpasses the wrestler of the Praisos plate (Fig. 29), and in his broad massive appearance introduces a new rendering of the body. And similarly the dog, coloured bright yellow with appropriate detail, goes far beyond the animal frieze style. One fancies that in this animal eagerly looking up to his master one sees expressed something like feeling.

Like the pinax of Timonidas many other votive tablets of the same find take one out of the stock vase scenes, especially in the delight in landscape, the trees conceived of in their special natures, the cross-section like genre scenes from the workshop of the potter and metal-worker, from mining and sea voyages. The vases, however, show little of those progresses in colouring and spacing, which we must assume in greater measure for the great art of painting. The decisive step in the history of vase painting, which is especially embodied for us by the painter Timonidas, con-sists in the liberation of the field, in the transition from the ornamental to the pictorial style, in the abandonment of filling ornamentation, which only survives in vegetable

46

motives suitable to the occasion and scattered birds, serpents, lizards(Figs. 34 and 66), and in the triumph of figure-subjects over friezes of ornament or animals, which can best be followed in the kraters (Fig. 65). With this step, which is completed in the beginning of the 6th century, we are brought close to the black-figured style proper, which is differentiated by some technical innovations.

But before we pass to that, we have still to follow the transition here described through the other fabrics of the 7th century. We can rapidly pass over Sparta, which as yet produces no ware fit for exportation. The course here is similar to what went on in the Argolid. Beside many specialities one seems to notice kinship with Ionian pottery in the small bands of squares accompanied by dots and the branches on the edge of the kylix, in the placing of similar animals in rows. In what close relation earlier Spartan civilization stood to Ionia, we learn from the history of lyric poetry.

To the three stages, earlier Protocorinthian, later Protocorinthian, older Corinthian, answer the three groups in Attica named respectively after Phaleron, the Nessos vase and Vurvá. The break-up of the most definite of all Geometric styles seems to have taken place in spite of vehement opposition. Details of the Oriental flora and fauna are first assimilated to the old style, and taken unobtrusively into the Geometric system of decoration. In the group named after the finds at Phaleron the new style with marked Phoenician imitations gets the upper hand. To the unsystematic reproduction and application of the new ornaments, now arbitrarily scattered, now ranged in special rows, and so added to the others, succeeds a severer choice, stylization and arrangement; the luxuriant vegetable character of the decoration (Fig. 46), with which birds and insects are often combined, only lasts for a time. The same experimental hesitation prevails in the figure drawing, which does not go straight from the Geometric silhouette to contour drawing and monochromy, but very soon experiments from time to time in the incised line and added white paint, and in the later Phaleron stage is not sparing of details in red, *e.g.*, for the hair and dress. The progress in the rendering of nature happily can still be followed to some extent in big vases. It leads to a fixed type with a loose outline with ankles, knee-pan, and elbow rendered like ornaments : in the head the big eye in front view dominates at the expense of the forehead, the skull is flat, the aquiline nose is very prominent, the ear is like a volute. Similarly in early Greek sculpture an ornamental conception of the outline and the details of the body is expressed, and casts a light on the conception of ornament as something living and not yet felt to be an abstraction from reality.

The big Phaleron vases also give evidence as to the grouping of the figures, which we have not been able to get from the Protocorinthian vases that have been preserved. Older specimens like the Berlin amphora from Hymettos already fill the greater part of the vase surface with the descriptive frieze, only surrounded by narrow lines of ornaments and animals, and in addition the neck of the amphora is adorned with figured scenes. Even in Geometric times Attic pottery had already given greater scope to the narrative style than other manufactures : in the Phaleron vases it creates an important system of decoration, which is continued in the group of which the Nessos vase is the chief representative, and prevails to the exclusion of everything else in the 6th century.

When the later Phaleron vases re-adopt the full silhouette in animal drawing and extend the technique of incised detail and additions in red to human outline figures, which they often emphasize only to make them stand out from the background, they prepare a step, which is completed in the Nessos group, *i.e.*, the taking over of the animal-frieze technique into figure-painting, with which vase-painting parts company again from the great art and returns to decorative silhouette effect. In Attica, too, the circular rendering of the eye is taken over for the male figure, the flesh-tone of the face is retained for decorative effect, women are distinguished by the old outline-drawing, decorative female creatures and monsters do not escape from the silhouette treatment (Fig. 48).

On vases of this technique the Orientalizing luxuriance developed out of Geometric richness is entered by a new spirit of severity and discipline, which one would be most inclined to explain by strong influence of Protocorinthian art. The field ornaments are similarly limited, and the rosette with points has the chief place; the lotus and palmette pattern of the Nessos vase (Fig. 48), the cable and the double rays of the Piraeus amphora (Fig. 49) are simple borrowings, the lion-type on the vase just named is closely connected with the Protocorinthian. One may ask whether the types in spite of their Attic stamp do not partly come from the Sicyonian-Corinthian school. The procession of chariots in the Piraeus amphora is only in the line of old tradition, but on the neck of the Nessos vase the Phaleron type is replaced by another, which is certainly only an extract from a larger composition, and the same artist makes the sisters of Medusa furiously pursue a Perseus not represented at all, whom the Aegina bowl of kindred style and the rather later cauldron in the Louvre show along with his protectors Athena and Hermes. At any rate the vase-painters had no hesitation in taking over the compositions once created and cutting them up, enlarging or abbreviating them according to their requirements, intensifying or weakening them according to their talents. The same

49

lucky ' laziness of invention ' is shown in the rendering of the individual figure. Old types of Oriental art are behind the battle motive of Herakles, the flight of the Gorgons, and the race of the Harpies on the Aegina bowl ; the unusual front view points to the origin of the Gorgon type as an ornament. But the Greek showed originality in animating and enhancing these types. In spite of the harsh perspective it is arrestingly expressive when the Medusa collapses in death, the sisters rush with the speed of lightning through the air, Herakles kicks the back of the rough monster, and the victim supplicates his tormentor by touching his beard : we have an art with the joy of youth full of vigour and possibilities of development displaying itself, the same early Attic art, which next found plastic expression in the early sculptures of the Acropolis. On the Nessos amphora the decorative figures are of secondary importance. The mouth bears the old goose frieze, the broad handles are adorned with owls and swans : under the principal field a row of dolphins gambol, but they are hardly to be conceived of as a meaningless animal frieze, but are to be understood in a ' landscape ' sense ; the wild chase is by sea. On the other vases of this group the animal frieze element is much stronger, on some it entirely prevails, e.g., on big-bellied amphorae with no angle dividing body from neck, and a bason from Vurvá, which both reduce the filling ornaments very considerably. These vases lead over to a noticeably miscellaneous class, the so-called Vurvá style, which just like the older Corinthian denotes a strengthening of the decorative and is also to be regarded as a rival of Corinth. The ornamentation is very limited, for filling there is nothing but rosettes, which may also form independent friezes : the decoration assumes quite similar forms to those of the Corinthian fabric. But the Corinthian elements do not entirely give its character to the Vurvá style. Apart

50

from the traditions of the brilliant Geometric period, which remained longer operative in the very ceramic and non-metallic Attic school than in the Argive-Corinthian, one suspects also influences from Eastern Greece. According to the evidence of vase finds, Athens was then in connection with Naukratis. Thus one may refer the painting of white on the figures, which is only occasionally employed at Corinth, but on the Vurvá vases often takes the place of the red, to the influence of the East, which had long known it, and explain in the same way many a similarity with the East in the motley array of animals.

Beside the common ware, purely decorative, technically trivial and poor, naturally the subject-vases went on, as at Corinth. It is not only the ' runners with bent knee ' mingled with the animals, the draped men and riders, who maintain the connection with the older figure-painting ; the traditions of the Nessos vase and its parallels continued on big and carefully executed vases. These vases are to Attic pottery, what the works of Timonidas were to Corinthian ; they give up filling ornament, individualize the world of figures out of its ornamental constraint, give the subject-style the spatial freedom, which it needs for its evolution. Just as we could follow this transitional style in Corinth on a vase and pinax of Timonidas, so it meets us in Attica at the same time in vases with decoration in bands, necked amphorae, kraters, and cauldrons, and in big-bellied amphorae with special field for the subject, which take the place, in some measure, of sepulchral votive 'pinakes,' and are decorated with a female bust or a horse's head, placed on a panel reserved in the black ground. This vase with special field, which arose from the needs of representation, only transitorily enters the service of animal decoration, and then becomes the chief vehicle of the new style, whose beginning we have reached with the last-named vases.

GREEK VASE-PAINTING

Attic pottery of the 7th century exercised great influence upon its Boeotian and Eretrian neighbours, where an independent artistic spirit never existed. One might describe these dependent manufactories as provincial branches of the Attic, had they not been influenced by other models as well. The big Boeotian amphorae with tall broad neck, the decoration of which consists chiefly of a pictorial frieze at the level of the handles, divided vertically, are imitated from vases of the islands (p. 25). The best known instance, from Thebes, shows on one side the Oriental goddess flanked by lions, on the other a flying bird and spiral ornamentation. This metope decoration with flying birds and Orientalizing volutes and palmettes called forth a special Boeotian class, which some conservative workshops went on producing with great tenacity to the end of the 6th century. It excels in tall-stemmed kylikes with white slip and colour accessories in red and yellow. Other workshops, like those of Pyros and Mnasalkes, imitated the Protocorinthian and Corinthian wares, quantities of which were imported; in the 6th century one enters an Attic sphere of influence. Similarly Attic and island influences are found side by side at the neighbouring Eretria in Euboea.

The Cycladic manufactory, to which the Boeotian and Eretrian imitations point, cannot yet be followed beyond the early Orientalizing stage. On the amphorae with white slip already described, to which class belongs the Stockholm vase with the roebuck (Fig. 50), and on the closely allied griffin jug from Aegina (Fig. 51), severely stylized flowers and tendrils enter the not very rich Geometric ornament, the new cable meets the old meander in the same frieze, rows of triangles are enclosed by spirals; in the metopes of the shoulder stripe appear, surrounded by scanty filling ornaments, simple animal representations, generally birds, also feeding animals, heraldic or fighting lions, pairs of panthers in heraldic scheme, in the characteristic partial silhouette, which renders the head and parts of the body in outline, but the skins with black or white spots according to the technique. The Ram jug from Aegina (Fig. 28), the exact attribution of which is uncertain, is at any rate closely allied.

This charming class has been called Euboic, but no Euboic find substantiates the name. It has hitherto come to light only on the islands of the Aegean ,especially Delos-Rheneia, Thera and Melos. Delos also supplied the earlier Geometric stages, but as the central meeting place of the islanders, it received so many different elements that it appears venturesome to rename the ' Euboic ' ' Delian ' ware, since a closely-allied pottery, which would have the same right to this name, can be probably distinguished from it. This class, which has a predilection for decoratively applied horse-heads, and like the Protocorinthian, has the habit of putting red and white stripes on parts of the vase which are covered with black, at an early date supplied figured representations without field ornaments ; it seems to have been occasionally imitated in the Euboic colony of Kyme, which otherwise is completely under Protocorinthian influence. The similarity of the animal representations to Cretan metal work and of the fine griffin head (Fig. 51) to those of bronze cauldrons from Olympia, strengthens the above-mentioned relations of the Euboic-Delian style to the Cretan and Argive.

Thera is not in question as the home of these vases. This island had its own very important fabrication in Geometric times, which like the Attic sticks obstinately for a long time to the old style, and as long as it exists, never allows the new elements, which often are strongly suggestive of metal patterns, to get the upper hand. In Melos it has been

E

perhaps correct to localize an important manufactory of which the products have been chiefly found in this island and in the neutral sphere of Delos-Rheneia. The heavy double spirals with gusset-like filling, which this style prefers to the other Orientalizing ornaments, and which it puts in to fill space, arranges in stripes, puts one on the top of another as ' the volute-tree,' or quadruples as ' the volute-cross,' give this pottery a peculiar stamp. The style is most finely represented by the big weighty amphorae which in shape and technique of the light ground for painting on are akin to the above-mentioned Cycladic vases, but are finely decorated on neck and body with representations, and also show the same feeling for rich decoration in the luxuriant filling ornamentation. The Melian delight in representation, like the Attic, gives us an insight into the growth of the figured style. The rows of geese (Fig. 52), the big sphinxes and panthers, the horses ranged heraldically on either side of a volute-cross, the favourite framed horse-busts show the well-known partial silhouette; and the female busts, the confronted riders, the duellists flanked by women, the gods facing each other or driving in chariots, the ' Persian Artemis ' carrying a lion, the free legendary scenes reflect in technique and drawing the same development which we followed at Athens. We can assign to about the date of later Phaleron vases a specimen like the Apollo vase (Fig. 52), which colours light brown the male body, and in the drawing of animals leads from the old partial silhouette to the later technique. The fine ' Marriage of Herakles ' (Fig. 53) marks a great step in advance, not only by the complete taking over of the black-figured animal style, and the superposition of many details in white on horses and patterns of garments, but above all by the lively rendering of the paratactic composition and the removal of all Geometric traces in the rendering of

54

bodies. The heraldic motives have given place to more natural ones ; the male type is not merely distinguished by brown painting from the female. The shape of the vase is more compact, the decoration more tectonic, the goose frieze on the shoulder edge is replaced by the tongue pattern, which also as garment edging drives out the old zig-zag. But the filling ornaments are as copious as ever, and the step, which the Nessos vase took in the technique of the figures, has not yet been taken. Thus the ' Melian ' vases take us lower down in the 7th century than the other Cycladic products, but not yet to its close.

Perhaps new finds will bring the continuation of these manufactories and build a bridge to the style of the 6th century. If we get them, we may hope for a completion of the picture here given, a clearing up of the relations of the manufactories to one another and to the East and West, and evidence as to their localization. For even the Melian origin of the ' Melian ' vases is not certain : this manufactory too, to judge by the chief locality of the finds, would have to be moved to Delos, the little inconspicuous island, where Leto bore her twins Apollo and Artemis, on which the whole Ionic world gathered to celebrate its divine fellow-citizens. We can trace something of this festal spirit and devotional pride of the insular Ionians in the Apollo and Artemis of the Melian vase, of course in a humbler way than in the magnificent hymn of the Ionian bard.

The technique of the white ground for painting and much in the filling ornament and the animal-drawing unites these insular vases with the artistic circle of S.W. Asia Minor and the adjacent islands, through which obviously, as well as through Crete, Oriental decorative motives principally found their way into Greece. The impulses which guided the weak Geometric style of this district into new paths can with certainty be traced to metal work, especially

Phoenician bowls, and to textile products. Miletus, the head of East Ionic civilization, had a flourishing textile industry in the 7th century, the decoration of which was quite under the spell of the East. An attempt has been made to fix at Miletus a manufactory, the extension of which coincides exactly with the commercial sphere of this great maritime town; the coast of Asia Minor and the adjacent islands, the colonies on the Black Sea and in the Delta are the most important, a secondary part is played by the Cyclades and the Italo-Sicilian area, but the Greek mainland is unaffected. But since Miletus need not have done more than distribute, just as Corinth did for the Protocorinthian ware, since closely allied and almost inseparable wares were made in several places, and the bulk of these vases were found in Rhodes, we may retain the traditional name ' Rhodian.'

The transition from the Geometric phase (p. 26) to the developed style of animal decoration can be to some extent followed. We see, for instance, the old shape of the jug (Fig. 22) become metallically rounded, the cable on the neck drive out the old zig-zags, and on the shoulder two animals antithetically flank the central metope (Fig. 54). The stiff division into metopes of the shoulder stripe is next dropped, the animals and fabulous beings of the East are placed heraldically one on either side of a central vegetable motive, and under this heraldic band, in obvious rivalry with textile work adorned in bands, continuous friezes of animals in rows, of dogs pursuing hares, of grazing wild goats and deer, of running goats, which in spite of their decorative character often testify to a very fresh observation of nature. Bands of different ornament, cables, and continuous loops, Geometric motives in metope-like arrangement, especially the upright garland of lotus buds and flowers, are added to the animal friezes : the last-named ornament generally takes the place of the rays round the bottom of the vase. With these decorative stripes the Rhodian style at the height of its production likes to cover the whole surface of its favourite jugs with ' rotelle ' on the handles (Figs. 55 and 56), its necked amphorae, bowls and other vessels, and in this way arrives at a delicate and rich carpet-like effect : the equipoise between the animal silhouettes neatly placed on the white ground, coloured red and white, and the vigorous clear ornamentation, the showing of the ground through in delicate details where colour is purposely omitted, the well-distributed filling ornaments, into which sometimes small birds with an absence of pedantry are introduced, are all very satisfactory to the decorative sense : the distinction of the shoulder stripe by the heraldic element prevents the impression that the surface of the vase is too uniformly cut up. The accumulation of animal friezes, and the heraldic arrangement of Orientalizing animals round a vegetable combination of ornaments, are features which we have already found in Western art ; but while these elements became prominent there at a time when the incised full silhouette was in exclusive possession of the field, when plant decoration took more abstract shapes, and filling patterns were reduced to the rosette, the culmination of the Rhodian animal-frieze vases falls in the pictorial period, when the plant decoration is naturalistic and filling ornamentation is abundant.

A uniform band decoration did not exclusively prevail. A group of jugs, which by its more tense and profiled shape and by a transition to the later floral ornamentation shows itself to be progressive, and which gradually replaces the cable of the neck by the broken so-called ' metope ' maeander (Fig. 56), leaves out of the black body of the vase only a narrow stripe with the maeander reduced to pothooks, and surrounds the bottom of the vase with long rays. But beside this method the other certainly persists. Its tenacious life is proved by vases like the Paris cauldron (Fig. 58) and its parallels from Naukratis, which show the archaic Rhodian band style alongside of the developed incised animal style on the same vase. In these hybrids which are essentially akin to the vases of Andokides (p. 115) the old stylizing of the figures is giving way, the rich store of filling motives is yielding to the prevalence of the rosette, the vegetable ornamentation is exchanging its vigorous plant-like appearance for thinner and more abstract shapes, which however take on a freer swing and submit to richer variations, the most important of which is the continuous tendril. At the same time the old technique of painting and leaving void spaces continues to be cultivated at a time, when elsewhere and probably also in the East the black-figured animal style has become the regular thing, and the filling ornamentation combined with it has assumed the blot-like shapes of the Corinthian and Vurvá stage. Finally the Rhodian style also adopts the new fashion.

Thus this style from an early date shows itself extremely decorative and little inclined to actual representations. We should know nothing of them, if the plates, a favourite item in Rhodian fabrication, like their Phoenician metal prototypes, did not exchange the old concentric decoration of stripes for the division into two segments, the larger of which is occasionally adorned with the human figure instead of the usual animal or fabulous creature. The drawing of the figures adopts the method already familiar. The place of outline drawing of the men is taken by brown tinting, e.g., in the heroes fighting in the well-known scheme on the Euphorbos plate (Fig. 57), while the women retain the old technique, e.g. the Gorgon on a plate in London, which is an adaptation of the Oriental animal goddess, and quite exceptionally fills the whole circular space (Fig. 59). Both plates show early beginnings of incised work, the Gorgon in the inner marking of the drapery, Hector's shield in the drawing of the flying bird. The view that the incised technique in figures is borrowed from Protocorinthian work receives support in this shield with its Argive suggestion, and in the Argive lettering, with which the excellent artist, roughly contemporaneous with the Chigi jug (Figs. 35 and 36), has transformed a conventional composition into a scene described in the 17th Book of the Iliad. The full silhouette with inner detail incised appears only in specimens, which from their degenerate filling ornaments are plainly late products of the 7th century, e.g. a plate with a running Perseus. That when this happens the eye retains its oval shape, is characteristic of the Eastern Ionic school.

This transition to the black-figured style can be better followed in a closely allied pottery, fixed by the contemporary inscriptions of dedicators to the Milesian colony of Naukratis in the Delta. While the old filling motives are coming to an end, and the vegetable stripe ornamentation is being increased by the addition of continuous tendrils and confronted lotus and palmette, and rows of circumscribed palmettes, of bands of buds and rows of pomegranates, the animal frieze adopts the incised full silhouette. The human representations, often of a high order of excellence, gradually asserting themselves beside the animal decoration, show a reluctance in taking this step. The old brush technique is still maintained in the specimens, which reserve thin lines in the silhouette instead of incising them (Fig. 60); and also the brown tinting of the male body (Fig. 61) seems to continue in this area longer than elsewhere. These conservative features are balanced by an innovation in colouring, which like the change in plant ornamentation denotes an important step to the style of the 6th century;

even before the actual decay of filling ornamentation, Naukratite painting (as in the Praisos plate, Fig. 29) begins to paint in white the light flesh of women, *e.g.* the face of the sphinx; and the same colour is used in the Herakles sherd (Fig. 61), on which the lion's skin still appears in the ground of the clay, in order to contrast with the linen jerkin.

The delight in polychrome effect is very strongly expressed on the interiors of the tall drinking cups and other vases, which the Naukratite painter likes to cover with a wash of black, and then to paint over it plant decoration in red and white. Incision enters also into their polychrome lotus decoration and thus gives it an effect similar to that of an older class of kylikes, big-bellied and necked amphorae, found in Rhodes, which is decorated in the old style with incised ornaments of red colour, and at a time when the Rhodian style was still practising pure brush technique, was already preparing for the later phase, a conclusion which must also be drawn from the Paris cauldron for animal representation. This black-ground polychromy, which occurs only occasionally on Rhodian jugs in white and red stripes, white rosettes and eyes (Fig. 55), becomes so popular and elaborate at Naukratis, that one is almost tempted to think of a continuation of Protocorinthian influence, since Naukratis was in close connection with Protocorinthian Aegina.

Beside Naukratis itself Aegina was also the chief place of export for this gaily coloured pottery, which unfortunately has only reached us in precious fragments, and of whose scenes of merry life drawn from legend, the revel and the dance we should gladly know more. With the Rhodian ware it also reaches Italy and Sicily; the Acropolis of Athens gives us, *e.g.* the fine Herakles sherd (Fig. 61), and Boeotia in a grave of the early 6th century a late cup with

60

heraldic cocks.

Beside the Rhodian ware Miletus seems also to have been the export-centre of another allied fabric, that of the vases called 'Fikellura,' from the name of the site in Rhodes, where they were first found. Their home is now generally sought in Samos because of the common ware found in that island. The greater number of the vases preserved, the prevalent form being the necked amphorae with metope-maeander (Fig. 56), are contemporaneous with the later phase of the Rhodian. This is proved by the advanced ornamentation with the thinner simplified lotus wreath, the rows of circumscribed palmettes, leaves (Fig. 63), pomegranates (Fig. 62), and crescents (Fig. 63) ; also by the almost complete disappearance of the 'horror vacui' so that the painter may reduce filling ornament to its lowest dimensions, paint big surfaces with loose net and scale patterns, and decorate the body of the vase with big continuous handle tendrils and an animal placed between them or only with a human figure boldly inserted in the void (Fig. 62). In the animals and fabulous beings, which add to the Rhodian types the heron and the water-hen or the fantastic man with the head of a hare, the partial silhouette is now rare; narrow lines left without colour, as at Naukratis, take the place of incised lines, and in the same technique are the purely human forms, which with their receding foreheads, projecting noses and almond-shaped eyes, with their coarse postures, are, like the Naukratis vases, true offspring of the Ionic spirit.

The Altenburg amphora (Fig. 63) must be a late example. The loin-cloths are painted red and framed with incised lines, which this style so long resisted. A few dot rosettes, reduced to their lowest dimensions, are all that is left of the old filling ornamentation, a long-stemmed bud, such as the early 6th century favours, projects into the field. Just as the runner of the London vase in his vigorous but stiff posture gives quite a new meaning to an old ornamental scheme, so the movements of the Altenburg revellers, which entirely fill the field, convince us of their intoxication. The ornamental style has now in the East, as well as in the West, become narrative and descriptive.

With these bibulous Ionians, who to the sound of flutes dance round their big mixing-bowl with cups and jugs, we pass finally from the wide ramifications of 7th century vase history to the developed archaic style.

CHAPTER IV.

THE BLACK-FIGURED STYLE

ARCHAIC art, the wonderful offspring of the contact of Greek civilization with the East, exercises its charm to-day more than ever. We have ceased to ascribe a unique saving grace to the classic period, the period of full bloom, and to allow no independent value to the preceding century except as an inevitable transitional phase. We love these archaic works of sculpture and painting for their own sake, not in spite of their crudities but just because of their unpolished hidden vigour, because of the precious combination of their essential features. The fetters of space, and the strong tradition of an ornamental early period give them a monumental effect, which has nothing of mummified stiffness but is kept ever fresh and youthful by an eminently progressive spirit and an energetic endeavour to attain freedom. The archaic style ' with fresh boldness goes beyond its Oriental patterns, is ever making fresh experiments, and thus exhibits constant change and progress. It is always full of serious painstaking zeal, it is always careful, takes honest trouble, is exactly methodical : the language which it speaks always tells of inward cheerfulness and joy at the result of effort, the effect produced by independent exertion. There is something touching in the sight of archaic art with its child-like freshness, its painstaking zeal, its reverence for tradition, and yet its bold progressiveness. What a contrast to Oriental and Egyptian art, which are fast bound in tradition : in the one the sweltering air of dull coercion, in the other the fresh atmosphere of freedom' (Furtwängler).

The history leading up to the origin of this style has become clear to us by quarrying in different localities. We saw the vases lose their peculiarly carpet-like appearance, the filling motives disappear, the bands of animals and ornaments forfeit their independence and become a subordinate member in the tectonic construction, we saw the world of figures win its way out of ornamental compulsion to greater freedom and extend over the vase. The 6th century, to the beginnings of which we pursued the history of vases, knows only occasionally inserted rosettes, or a lonely bud projecting into the field. Plant ornamentation becomes true Greek ornament, abstract, tectonic, and when occasion demands, full of life with its swing. Animal friezes retire to the foot or the shoulder, are often incidentally treated as mere decorative accessories or seized by quite unheraldic liveliness. The principal interest is devoted to depicting man, his doings and goings on. The vase painter is now more anxious than ever to narrate and depict; he finds ever less satisfaction in ornamental composition. He is never tired of describing hunting and warfare, wrestling and chariot-racing, the festal dance and procession, but with greatest preference, remembering the purpose of his vases, drinking and wild dancing. But also the heroes of past ages, their bold exploits and strange adventures, are his constant theme. The Homeric Epic, the tales of Herakles the mighty, the bold Perseus and Bellerophon, had evoked pictorial representations even in the 7th century; but now the full stream of the legendary treasury pours into painting and gives an infinitely rich material to the joy of narration.

What the vase-painter makes of this material is never conceived in the historical or archæological spirit, but breathes entirely the air of his own time; often only the added names (which according to the new feeling for space assume smaller dimensions) raise a genre scene into one from myth. Moreover the Saga is only seldom re-shaped by inventive brains. Types once invented pass on, go from workshop to workshop, from one district to another, are abbreviated (p. 49), expanded, conventionally repeated or filled with new life. Types may also cross; there arise purely through art, contaminations of legend, which are foreign to poetry. When a Corinthian painter unites the Embassy to Achilles (Iliad IX) with the visit of Thetis, this has as little to do with poetry, as when on Attic vases the birth of Athena is coupled with the apotheosis of Herakles, or the slaying of Troilos is transferred to Astyanax, or the entombment of the dead Sarpedon to Memnon. But everything strange need not be misunderstanding on the artist's part. The vases supply us with a multitude of legendary motives and variations, which we cannot find in literature, and are the faithful reflex of the fluidity of Greek mythology, which, devoid of canon and dogmatism, was in constant flux.

Olympos too, is subject to these vicissitudes. Its gods live a human life among men, the only difference being that some representative scenes give them a stiffer and more elaborate appearance than that of ordinary mortals. In early times the divinity is chiefly betokened by inscriptions and attributes. On the painting of the Corinthian Kleanthes stood Poseidon with a fish in his hand beside Zeus in labour. Late observers of this picture failed to understand this external characterization of the sea-god, and saw an act of brotherly sympathy with the god's pains in this holding up of the tunny; and thus a great deal beside must have appeared strange to them, e.g. Apollo with the great lyre still bearded in the 7th century (Fig. 52), Herakles without lion-skin (Fig. 64), the unarmed Athena, who only at the beginning of the 6th century, in contrast with the Chigi vase (Fig. 37), the Aegina bowl and the Gorgon lebes (p. 49), begins to express her bellicose nature by attributes, and much besides.

The favourite god of the drinking vessels is the wine-god with cup and vine. He makes Hephaistos drunk and leads him back to Olympos to liberate Hera from the magic chair. The big-bellied dancers and purely human creatures, who form his escort on Corinthian vases, in the first third of the century are superseded by the Ionic horse-men, the Satyrs, who become ever more closely associated with Dionysos, celebrate feasts with the Maenads, never despise the gifts of their master, and make fair nymphs pay for it. The half-bestial creature in whom ancient Greek fancy vigorously incorporates man's pleasure in wine and women with all its comic effects, is quite the patron of archaic vase-painting.

That all these representations were developed by vase-painting alone is more than improbable. That the Bacchic scenes of toping and dancing were created on the actual vase, is most likely; but one is often enough compelled to assume other sources. The fight of Herakles with the lion, for instance, in its oldest form is the borrowing of an Oriental type, which is composed for a tall rectangle, and is expanded by the vase-painters for their purposes by filling figures, 'spectators.' The gifted artist, who gave this heraldic type the more natural impress which was regular in the older black-figured style, was perhaps a vase-painter; the creator of the later black-figured type was certainly not, for his horizontal group is certainly a fine invention but always has to be adapted artificially to the vase surface. As with the wrestling of Herakles, so it is with Theseus' struggle with the Minotaur. The same sort of extension occurs on a favourite subject of older black-figured style, the quadriga in front view, whose horses heraldically turn their heads sideways, whose helmeted warrior is in front view while the unhelmeted driver is in profile. This type, certainly invented for a square, is also known in bronze and stone relief, and the question, in what technique it first appeared, will scarcely be answered in favour of vase-painting. For a square, too, the finely compact group of Herakles wrestling with Triton was first composed, a theme common on Attic vases from the hydria of Timagoras onwards; the older wrestling scheme, superseded by this type, in its Herakles spread out before the eyes of the observer and kneeling as he wrestles, still shows strong affinity with the Orientalizing frieze compositions (p. 46), and is for vase decoration much more typical than the later invention, which on vses always has a 'borrowed' effect. The dependence of vase-painting on other techniques is finally evidenced by the so-called 'couplings': the best-known instance is the combination of the departure of Amphiaraos with the Funeral-games of Pelias on a Corinthian (Fig. 66), an Attic and an Ionic vase, a combination which is borrowed from an inlaid wooden chest of Corinthian workmanship at Olympia ('the chest of Kypselos') or a prototype from which both were derived.

After all this one will not hesitate to look for a strong reflex of the great art of painting on the vases, alongside of the special property of the vase-painter and typical ornamental figures equally common to all art, or to picture to oneself wall-paintings or easel pictures, like the birth of Athena by Kleanthes, after the fashion of the best vase-paintings, which are least constrained by ornamental considerations, or to reconstruct from the copies of vase-painters compositions like the Destruction of Troy (Iliupersis), the Return of Hephaistos, the Reception of Herakles into Olympos. One is particularly impelled this way, when the vases give now shorter, now longer, extracts from the same large composition ; thus we have a reflection on some dozen vases of Exekias and his successors of the fine representation of the heroes Aias and Achilles surprised by the Trojans while deeply absorbed in a game of draughts, and warned by Athena just in time (Fig. 96). One cannot conceive of any difference of principle in perspective, in the rendering of the body and the drapery, in the spiritual content, between vase-painting and free painting ; they both are children of one time. Nor did the vase-painter feel any necessity to alter the composition of his patterns. Only as he had to decorate framed bands, the law of isocephalism was more binding for him than for the great art. Hence his strong disinclination for "landscape," which we often meet with in Corinthian and Ionian pinakes and wall-painting, but on the vases never, or only in palpable caricature ; the painter who on a hydria from Caere copied a seascape with the Rape of Europa, was obliged to place beside the figure what looks like a mole-hill but is intended for a mountain.

This limitation of the possibilities of composition by decorative considerations was of hardly any importance. The wide gulf between free painting and vase picture was conditioned in the first instance by technique. It was that which gave its special effect to the black-figured style and set its stamp upon it. We saw previously that vase-painting, when it took over the silhouette style from the decorative animal frieze, increased its distance from free painting, under whose spell it had been for a good part of the 7th century, that with the incised technique it took over, e.g. the circular drawing of the eye, and with the new colouring entered decorative paths (pp. 38, 44, 49). Free painting drew with the brush on light ground, used black and white very sparingly, more frequently red, blue, green, yellow and brown; placed these colours side by side in simple harmonies, with very little gradation and shading, but also sometimes, *e.g.* to represent fire, used the smooth brush; rendered the men in reddish brown, women, children, animals and objects in light colouring. With this free-coloured effect the black-figured style was neither able nor anxious to compete. Just like the Geometric, it is in its own fashion again an ornamental style, which does not dis-own its predominantly decorative character. The figure silhouettes serve it as ornaments to fill a given space, which are in a certain equipoise of colour in relation to the rest of the decoration and the black painted parts of the vase; the incision stipulates a sharp delineation of types, the imposed colour gives a parti-coloured effect. The coloured effect of the vases is essentially defined by the clay, which now, in the developed black-figured style, takes on a brilliant warm red upper surface, and by the black glaze, which assumes a metallic lustre. The darker colouring of the clay deprives the lighter parts of their effects by contrast, and compels the painters to replace the contour-drawing of women, linen garments, etc., gradually by laying on white colour, with which at first the contour is simply filled; but afterwards more commonly black underpainting is overlaid. With the transition to white, clear silhouettes are also obtained, which set off against the background more effec-tively than the old contour figures.

The advance in the preparation of the clay and glaze colour came about on the Greek mainland. Tradition makes the Sicyonian Butades invent the red colouring of the clay at Corinth, and thus gives the correct indication. The Chalcidian and Attic workshops helped the new technique to prevail; in the East it gradually gets the upper hand and forces the Ionian manufactories to give up their favourite white ground and adapt their technical freedom to the growing strictness of the western system. Attica, which in the 6th century opens a dangerous rivalry in Eastern and Western markets and finally wins the day, brings the process to perfection. With the refinement of incised technique it puts an end to the parti-coloured method still much affected by Corinthians and Chalkidians, it clears away the big surfaces coloured red and white and all colour in ornament and animal frieze, and helps the harmony of clay and black to its purest and fullest effect.

With the disappearance of the old parti-coloured system the vases are completely removed from the effect of free painting. For that we may be grateful to fortune. For this refinement of the black-figured style permitted the sensitive feeling of Greek artists for decoration to satisfy the delight of narrating and describing along with the ornamental traditions of the old style. They had no need, as had the old Minoan vase-painters (p. 10), to shrink from borrowing figured scenes. The recasting of types into the decorative silhouette style made it possible for them to conjure on to the vases whatever touched their hearts and delighted their eyes, and thus to transmit to us an infinite variety of scenes, without which our knowledge of Greek legend, Greek life and Greek art would have remained terribly scanty.

Corinth must lead off the history of this new style. The chief centre of commerce and industry in the Peloponnese, the celebrated seat of a flourishing ceramic industry and of an important school of painting, it not only took the decisive step to the new technique, but even in its red-clay phase had helped the designs to drive out animal decoration, and composed, or at least introduced into vase-painting, numerous types, which supply material to other workshops for a long time. The quadriga in front view, which Chalcidian and Attic painters repeated so often and which kept its decorative effect for almost a century, appears here for the first time ; the triangular scheme of two wrestlers seizing each other by the arms and pressing head against head, which survived to the time of Nikosthenes, was taken by the Amphiaraos krater (Fig. 66) from the above-mentioned chest of Kypselos (p. 67) ; the nuptial procession of Peleus and Thetis which we shall meet on the lebes of Sophilos and the François-vase is prepared for in Corinthian vase-painting ; and the battle-scenes, rider-friezes and chariot-races, of which there was a beginning in the Protocorinthian style, were most richly developed by the Corinthians, and adopted by Chalkis and Athens often without any essential improvement. Thus one may be sure, that a number of other types, which are not represented in the selection that accident has given us, started their victorious career from Corinth, and that the lost great art of Corinth, the bronze industry of which we have specimens and the richly-adorned chest of Kypselos described by Pausanias supplied to the vase-painters a number of mythological compositions, which influenced other manufactories. Unfortunately the greater part of this rich treasure is lost to us. The loss is the more to be lamented, as what we have shows us a fine inventive talent on the part of the Corinthian artists and a magnificently free and easy conception of life and legend. The Homeric poetry and the Epic inspired by it, the lays of Peleus and Herakles, the ballad poetry now becoming very fashionable, from which come *e.g.* the birth of Athena and probably also the Return of Hephaistos to Olympos, are reflected on these Corinthian vases in inimitably vivid and drastic fashion ; and the vase-painter also gives scenes from daily life, carouses, drunken men who dance wildly with naked women, kitchen and wine-press, riding and driving, marching out to battle, and the wild mellay itself. It is particularly on the kraters (Figs.

64-66) that we can trace how the accumulating material gets space on the vases; animal decoration, in which heraldic cocks are very popular, retires ever more to the reverse, under the handles, into the base stripe, and also by preference is replaced by lines of galloping riders, who form a lively decorative foil to the mythological principal picture (Fig. 64). Meanwhile filling ornament disappears. The flying bird over the rider (Fig. 65) renders the same service as the rosette, nay a better; it transplants the scene out of a decorative space into an actual one, the open country; and the space-filling animals of the Amphiaraos vase, which are traditional (p. 40), are not intended merely any longer to enliven the vase surface but the wall of the house, the floor and the air. Thus the liberation of the field, for which Timonidas and his fellows paved the way, is attained. With this goes hand in hand the liberation of figure-drawing from ornamental constraint. The outspreading of the figure in the surface, which is still strong in the 7th century, is toned down or ingeniously given a motive, as with the kneeling warrior who fights backwards, and does not disguise his connection with the old runner with bent knee. The individualizing of men and animals carried forward by Timonidas now once more makes big advances in human figures, horses and dogs.

We will select two of the kraters to give us an idea of the development of the style. One, a Paris vase (Fig. 64), gives a special application to a fine banqueting scene, by added names and the insertion of Iole, as the visit paid by Herakles to Eurytios, king of Oichalia. The fair daughter of the house stands with some indifference between the guest and her brother; it is supposed to represent a legend, but is really little more than a genre scene, as which it is hard to beat. The lively conversation of the guests, the dogs tied to the sofa-legs waiting and speculating on the chance of

72

bits falling from the table are masterly, and even the horses in the supporting frieze, if out of proportion and inelegant, are the more characteristic and living. The technique follows old tradition ; the flesh of Iole, tables and sofas, one dog, shields on the reverse, appear in outline drawing. Such contours, also found sometimes where men's bodies left white set off those painted dark, unite to some extent, as does the red colouring of the male countenance, the vase in its effect with the great art.

On the other hand the Amphiaraos krater (Fig. 66), which gives up red for male faces, and makes a point of covering the outline figures with a layer of white, has become more decorative and black-figured. Its pictures are not equal in execution to the invention, but come from excellent models (p. 67). Between the colonnade and façade of the house, which are in line like the tables in the Eurytios vase, the hero, because of his oath, mounts his chariot to go with open eyes to the death he forebodes ; his angry look is directed to Eriphyle and the fatal necklace in her hand. With raised hands the family takes leave, a maid-servant gives the stirrup-cup to the charioteer. Foreboding evil, the faithful Halimedes sits on the ground : his heart has evidently bidden him to train up the boy Alkmaion to take vengeance on his mother. The whole delight in narration, which in the exaggerated rendering of the necklace strongly emphasizes the previous history, is as genuinely archaic, as the mythological individualizing of an old type 'The warrior's departure.'

The Amphiaraos krater is more developed than the Eurytios vase, not merely in technique. The painter of the later vase, though not so gifted as his colleague, draws more cleverly, and works with a set of types before him, as the frieze of riders shows. The advance becomes plain in the shape of the vase. The Eurytios krater encloses an almost uniformly swelling cauldron between a lip ring which is very low and a foot which spreads out in ample dimensions. From this round-bellied archaic shape we pass to a later more defined and elegant one in the Amphiaraos krater, which has a higher neck, a steeper and much less swelling body, with its lower part running to a point, till finally the outline almost resembles an inverted triangle and from the handles a rectangular or curved bridge has to be built leading to the high rim (krater a colonnette). The tendency to development, which we can read out of the vase shapes, may be taken as a symbol of the history of style. For a Greek vase was always something organic, as much so as a tree or animal.

Unfortunately, besides the large kraters with their numerous figures, which were favourite articles of export, few vases are preserved. In the scene on the Eurytios krater we get the lebes with stand, also the jug and drinking cup (kylix), which exist in various extant specimens. The kylix has an offset lip (as in Fig. 24), and often knobs on the handles, the interior picture is framed by tongue pattern. Beside the necked amphorae, which like the kraters seldom have any other ornament than rays, shoulder tongues and neck rosettes, the similarly decorated big-bellied amphorae continue, which like their Attic parallels (p. 51) put human busts or animal representations of old and new style into the figure panel. The three-handled water pitcher (hydria) has the type with vaulted shoulder common in the older black-figured style, and adorns it with spirals and maeanders. All these ornaments, to which may be added the double lotus and palmette of the Eurytios krater and occasional net and step patterns, partake of the solidity and variety of the style.

Strangely enough, the phase of the Corinthian style here described is for us the end of the fabric; not one of these vases can be dated below the first third of the 6th century. Corinthian pottery has no share in the Eastern Herakles with the lion-skin, the Amazons as Scythian women, the entry of the Satyrs, the rendering of folds, the painted ground for white additions. One asks whether this brilliant development could break off so abruptly, or if it is only accident which has concealed from us its continuation. Both are improbable. It looks rather as if, just as the Proto-corinthian manufactory had its continuation in the Corinthian, so the Corinthian was carried on by the Chalkidian. For the vases denoted by their inscriptions as Chalkidian form, at all events according to the present state of our knowledge, a group covering a few decades, which is in succession of time to the later Corinthian vases, and is most closely connected with them by a series of detailed agreements. Not only do the vase shapes consistently carry on Corinthian tendencies, but details of decoration like the white neck rosettes filled with red, and the step pattern (Figs. 68 and 69) continue ; the Corinthian animal friezes with rosettes, the heraldic cocks, with the serpents, the winged demon, the riders with the space-filling birds (Fig. 69), the wrestlers scheme, the grotesque dancers, the quadriga in front view are taken over ; nay, details of drawing, like the warrior's head in front view, the round outline of the edge of the short small chiton (Figs. 70 and 71), the red spots on black clothes (Fig. 70), the sword sheath with the St. Andrew crosses (Fig. 71), the devices on the shields are not conceivable without their Corinthian predecessors ; even the names of Corinthian grotesque dancers pass over to the Chalkidian Satyrs.

Not a single Chalkidian vase has been found in Chalkis itself, nor even in any part of the mother-country : all specimens preserved come from the West. One might therefore assume that the fabric had its seat, not in Chalkis itself, but in one of its colonies, and thus the powerful Corinthian traditions in this pottery would be easily explained. The West was dominated, as we saw, throughout the 7th century by Corinthian exportation ; and the colonies of Chalkis had always been provided by friendly Corinth with clay vases. But the strong influence of the Chalkidian manufactory on the Attic is in favour of Chalkis itself having put an end to Corinthian production, or at any rate to Corinthian exportation. Why and how, cannot be stated : perhaps the publication of the many unpublished specimens will solve the riddle and clear up the close relation of the Chalkidian ware to the group of the Phineus kylix (Fig. 74).

From every point of view the Chalkidian vases give us a heightening of the Corinthian, a great advance in the direction of a later period. Clay and black now attain their highest perfection, the distribution of colour is most delicately calculated ; no longer is there so much use made of white surfaces (under which there is regularly a wash of black) ; especially we see no more of the arbitrary colour-contrast which did not shrink from white colouring of the male. If the Corinthian style had already aimed at metallic effect in the angular formation of the handles and the curving of the handle-bridges of the krater, the Chalkidian heightens these tendencies almost to faithful copying of metal vases, and consistently develops the vase shapes to the highest, almost over-refined elegance ; the narrowing of the lower part of the body leads to the insertion of a roll, which the painter picks out in red from the black foot. Thus arise novel vase-shapes ; the necked amphora (Fig. 69) is elongated, its shoulder flattened, so that the body almost assumes the shape of an egg ; the krater gets steep sides, high neck, and outward-bent handle bridges ; out of the older hydria with arched shoulder comes a later shape, which, in a specimen at Munich (Fig. 68) exactly copies the addition of cast handles to a metal body ; and similarly the other shapes develop, the kylix with knobs on the handles, the two-handled cup, the jug.

The same endeavour after elasticity and elegance prevails in the distribution of the ornament over the vase, which was managed in a more masterly way at Chalkis than elsewhere. Certainly the ornamentation is based almost entirely on Corinthian foundations. The white dot-rosettes filled with red on the black neck, the lotus and palmette on the ground of the clay, tongues on the shoulder, and rays at the foot, the step pattern under the chief frieze are of old tradition but pass through a growing elaboration. As a new motive of decoration comes in the chain of buds, which we know from the East : as a rule it occurs beneath the chief band (Fig. 69), or hangs over the figure-field in place of the lotus and palmette. The Ionic pattern is not exactly imitated in the process ; the swellings under the Chalkidian buds suggest roses rather than lotus. Out of these buds, palmettes, and the tendrils uniting them, is formed the fixed ornament, which generally serves as central motive to heraldic animals and often develops into a wonderfully rich complex of lively lines (Fig. 69). The proper place for this ornament is the centre of the upper band, which recovers its importance, now that the shoulder is set off more sharply in hydriae and necked amphorae, and as secondary field for decoration is, like the reverse of vases, usually decorated in the first instance with animals. On the shoulder-stripe the riders with the space-filling birds tend to drive out the archaic scheme of decoration ; they flank the lotus and palmette cross and in later specimens, where the horizontal shoulder is no longer dominant in the general view, they pass from heraldic constraint to parade order, and are also occasionally replaced by cleverly disposed dancers. The reverse of the vase also more and more shakes off animal decoration and replaces it by ornamental compositions, as by the heraldic quadriga or the heraldic riders. Friezes of animals beneath the main scene (Fig. 68) become very rare. However markedly the decoration of the vase departs from the old style, yet in spite of that there is in contrast with the Corinthian style a marked decorative invasion to be traced. The vases that have nothing but animal decoration are numerous, and the rosette often asserts itself again.

This decorative invasion, which is connected with the perfection of technique and marked talent of the Chalkidian artizan, does not detract in any way from the figure scenes. The latter preserve their old vigour and power of observation, some masters even raise it to a most intense elasticity, and breathe into the old types a new and vivid life, which in union with the fine technique and arrangement in space makes these vases superior to most of the other black-figured pottery. How Herakles on the London amphora (Fig. 70) unmercifully deals the death-blow to the three-bodied Geryon, or on the similar Munich vase (Fig. 71) to Kyknos, is brought before our eyes with unambiguous matter-of-fact and verve.

The chest of Kypselos had already thus represented Herakles' fight with Geryon, and the Chalkidian painter rests here, as often and especially in his battle scenes, on Corinthian types. But his rendering is anything but a borrowing, and bears witness to fresh and vigorous conception. The 'Herakles and Kyknos' is based on the old fighting scheme, which represents a warrior with raised right arm assailing an opponent who almost kneeling moves to the right but looks round ; and so in effect only combines the ' duellist ' (p. 39) and the runner with bent knee. On the Chalkidian picture the old ' exigency of space ' type is hardly any longer to be traced ; everything has become expressive and characteristic. To be sure the contrast between the body in front view and the legs in profile and the spreading over the surface are still hardly toned down, but the thrust dealt with the right arm, the clutch of the left, the foot pressed against the back of the opponent's knee are full of vigour, and the collapse of the bleeding son of Ares, his prayer for mercy while he plucks the victor's beard, the dimmed eye with its pathos, the composition and the filling of the space are very artistic.

This heightening of characteristic touches does not merely appear in battle scenes, but also the intimate touches in many Corinthian subjects are carried on. Even the Eurytios krater had succeeded in expressing the horror which seizes Odysseus and Diomede at the sight of the suicide of Aias. The feeling in this group is perhaps surpassed by an episode in a Chalkidian battle-scene; where the intent care, with which Sthenelos binds up the finger of the wounded Diomede, reminds one of the later kylix of Sosias (Fig. 114); and when a Paris amphora enlarges the march out to battle by a domestic scene of arming, early red-figured painting is again anticipated.

The combination of this fresh and direct observation of nature with a marked decorative talent unites Chalkidian with the Ionic art of the islands. On Chalkidian soil, where a language with a strong Ionic element was spoken, a close contact with eastern neighbours must be assumed. It is not only the chain of buds on the vases that witnesses to this contact. The Satyr, a hairy fat fellow, with marked horse-ears and horse-tail, often with horse-hoofs, enters from the East in a form, which meets us on the Phineus vase (Fig. 74). And when the Chalkidian painter occasionally indicates the outline of the female back, where previously the drapery falling straight down entirely concealed it, when he furnishes his Geryon with wings and often equips Herakles with the lion's skin, in this, as in much besides, one cannot fail to see Eastern influence. Whether the rendering of folds, the beginnings of which appear on Chalkidian vases as elsewhere, has the same origin, is doubtful.

The fabric in the Ionic islands which was in close reciprocal relation with the Chalkidian, may be called the ' Phineus ' fabric after its chief product, till accident betrays to us its home. From the remains of lettering on the Phineus kylix, it can only be said, that it was produced in a place where Ionic was spoken, which cannot have been near to Asia Minor. The style, more Eastern than Chalkidian, but different from East Ionic in much, *e.g.* the circular drawing of the male eye, and closely akin to Chalkidian, is probably of Cycladic origin. But a connection of this pottery with one of the old Cycladic manufactories (p. 52) is impossible. As little as the Chalkidian has it any previous history ; the few amphorae and kylikes that remain belong exactly to the same short period of time, in which the Chalkidian vases were produced.

The amphorae are rather earlier than the Phineus vase, and often very like the decorative earlier Chalkidian specimens. Chalkis seems to have supplied to them the western technique, the vase-shape, the foot-ring, and also to have supplied the patterns in many specimens for animal and rider decoration. But the less severe construction of the vases, the irregular division of the fields for figures, the preference for a dark covering of the ground above the rays, the liberties in decoration, lead us to more Eastern soil. The very chain of buds, luxuriant and hardly stylized, which often covers the neck, shows the unpedantic and concrete Ionic style, and the same playful carelessness appears, when the painter is lavish with filling rosettes and buds, when he inserts into a heraldic frieze of animals a complex of creatures furiously biting each other, or puts between his favourite squatting sphinxes a fighting warrior, a couple of dancers, or two running girls, when he composes heraldically the heads of two processions of riders, and makes a combatant the central motive of heraldic riders, when he invents animal combinations with a common head. So it is no wonder if he makes into an effective motive of decoration the apotropaic eyes popular in this phase of art, which we know from Delian, Melian, and Rhodian vases of the 7th century (Fig. 57), if he often adds ears and nose, and fills the centre with an arbitrarily chosen motive, a leaf or a human figure. The eyes are found on the necks of amphorae, but very often as outside decoration of the kylix, which in perfected specimens shows alike the height and the end of this manufacture.

The wonderfully living and swelling outline of these delicate kylikes (Fig. 72) may be taken as a symbol of the style of the figures, which is absolutely remote from abstract dryness. It often enough adopts Corinthian-Chalkidian types as models. The ' Phineus ' painter did not invent of himself the warrior with head in front view ; the slaying of Troilos goes back to an old Corinthian type ; the pursuit of the mounted Penthesileia introduces, it is true, a new Eastern Amazon·type in place of the old one (which is also used in this group), but is based on the composition of a Corinthian battle picture. What the ' Phineus ' painter does with his models is always distinguished by individual and genuinely Ionic life. On the group of amphorae a fine vigorous figure style prevails, which on the kylikes has a finer and at the same time more delicate development. The charming Athena (Fig. 73), who now appears in armour, and whose shield-edge the painter for decorative reasons has doubled, the Scythian who like the mounted Amazon is at home in East Greece, the skipping Silenus, the dog in front view would not tell us much of this kylix-style. But fortunately the painter of the Phineus kylix surrounded the fine Silenus mask in the interior with a continuous frieze, the lack of which a hundred contemporary vases could not outweigh. The wall with the vine and the lion's head plainly divides the frieze into two scenes: evidently a magic well, which pours wine into the cup of the delighted Satyr. A lion, a panther and two stags draw the chariot of the Wine-god and his consort. On the legendary team a Satyr is making mischief; two of his colleagues are quite diverted from their duty by the sight of three nymphs, who are bathing at a spring in a wood. A lion's head as spout pours into a basin the water with which they are laving themselves; their clothes they have already hung up. The other picture shows the blind king Phineus, from whom the Harpies have taken the food off the table, for which he is vainly feeling; the valiant sons of Boreas pursue the impudent thieves through the air over the sea.

All is living, original and drastic in its conception, as perhaps was only possible for an Ionian. The movements of the Satyrs and the nude maidens, the animals and plant-life are caught from nature, and this study betrays itself in various details. The face of Phineus, still painted red like that of the Satyrs, is drawn in front view, which we have hitherto only found in the helmeted warrior's head, the collar-bone and chest muscles are rendered, the eyes of the Boreads are already much reduced in scale. Especially important is the treatment of the drapery, not to mention the linen chiton of Dionysos with its parallel lines indicating the material, or the long red chitons of the women and the curved outline of the shirts of the Boreads, or the garments of the Harpies adorned with Ionic crosses and borders; important innovations appear in the himatia, that of Phineus is divided into red and black stripes, those of Dionysos and the women show rendering of folds. That the himation rather emphasizes than conceals the outline of the back, is a true Ionic feature.

Beyond this stage, the ' Phineus ' fabric cannot be traced. Generally the Cycladic pottery of this period is hard to get hold of. We do not know whether there were more factories on the islands, and some isolated but allied specimens with more fully Ionic alphabet cannot yet be localized. On the other hand, the ceramic history of the Greek East offers at least some fixed points, though the transition from the old style has not yet been cleared up. We were able to accompany the Rhodian-Naukratite and the ' Fikellura ' styles to the very threshold of the black-figured, but here the thread seems to snap. Shallow bowls found in Egypt and South Russia with bud decoration and black-figured interior designs, which were imitated by the Attic Vurvá style, and amphorae with remains of the old ornamentation and big isolated animal-silhouettes in the field, perhaps represent the latest products of the Rhodian style. The ' Fikellura ' style finds its continuation in a ware, which was certainly produced in Klazomenai, perhaps also in several places at the same time, and has come to light not only in the Ionian region and the colonies in Egypt and the Black Sea, but also in Italy. The Klazomenian style has in common with its predecessor not only a series of ornaments (tongues, rays, late Rhodian garlands, continuous tendrils, rows of crescents, friezes of leaves, ' metope ' maeanders, buds in the field, scales over a surface), but continues the old shape of amphora and has the same preference for loose decoration : beside the vases adorned in bands, on which the animal friezes are driven out of the chief band, it is very fond of a field consisting of a reserved panel or running all round, and of the decoration

83

of the neck by means of an ornament, an animal head or a human head. In the field it likes to put instead of the heraldic pair a single animal, a sphinx before a standing man or upright branch, an isolated palmette and lotus cross, which are in a measure constituent parts of heraldic compositions, and shows the same freedom, going even beyond that of the Phineus painter, when it makes isolated figures, dancers, running girls, or men wearing mantles, the central motive of its heraldic sphinxes or cocks, and when it puts a runner with bent knee between two lions that turn away from him (Fig. 75). The palmette and lotus-cross and the animal types differ from Western types; the selection, too, is characteristic of the East. There is a special preference for the Siren: this bird-woman is used surprisingly often heraldically, and in rows to make a frieze. The female panther occurs as well as the male; the grazing deer is a Rhodian legacy. The ostriches show knowledge of Africa, the winged horses and boars connection with Asiatic art. The Klazomenian style is particularly strong in the new formation of fantastic beings, to which the near neighbourhood of the East gave the impulse. The sea-horse and the Triton were invented somewhere in this area: to the ' Fikellura ' man with the head of a hare Klazomenai adds a being with a tail and a lion's head among human revellers, among dancing men and women appears suddenly the bearded monster with the horse's tail, the Satyr (Fig. 75).

The stock of types varies considerably from that of the West; this is particularly clear in the scenes with human figures. Beside the pictures of riders and battles, beside the few preserved legendary scenes, among which the most important are the battles of Amazons, who here in the East have become mounted Scythian women, the prominent place is taken by scenes of drinking and dancing in the manner of the Altenburg amphora (Fig. 63). The file principle, so potent in the East Ionic animal frieze, strongly asserts itself in the dancing maidens and the abandoned revellers : the oblique inclination forward, which the Klazomenian painter often gives the intoxicated, and which is very successfully preserved on an early Milesian relief in London, emphasizes at the same time the decorative arrangement, and increases the expressiveness, just as the eccentric movements of the dancers equally well fill the space and mark the tone. For life, sensual and everyday though often grotesque and brutal, is what these Ionian masters give, even if they are only decorative artists or artizans, whatever it may cost. So they succeed in nothing so well as women, satyrs and animals. The maidens with their receding foreheads, almond-shaped and often obliquely set eyes, and the little mouth somewhat drawn in below, and the well-marked back contour, have an attractiveness even on the most careless representations ; the shaggy satyrs betray their equine nature not merely in ear, tail and hoof ; the robust strong-maned horses, the female panthers with swelling breasts, the fighting cocks forgetting their heraldic duties, all show nature very close at hand.

The history of this style, which must approximately extend over the first half of the 6th century, can be to some extent followed. In the beginning comes the conflict of the old Ionic and Western techniques, the transition from the light slip to the reddish-yellow surface, and the tendencies in ornamentation which still strongly remind one of ' Fikellura.' The silhouette style makes liberal use of white. Not only with inherited aversion does it often replace incision by delicate lines of paint, provide garments with white crosses, animals with white spots and white belly-stripe, and ornaments with white details : in its earlier period it also extends the white surfaces, which it still places

85

6

on the ground of the clay at times, from women and linen chitons to men, horses and dogs, and becomes as parallel to the Corinthian style with this contrast of colouring as with its wide-necked broad-bellied form of amphora.

The latest wares of the colony of Daphne (abandoned in 560 B.C.) show the transition to the rendering of folds of drapery, which takes the place of the old parti-coloured surfaces in the group of vases which took its rise about the middle of the century. In this later group, to which a series of ' lebetes ' with topers, satyrs, centaurs, and battle scenes is an obvious introductory link, and which culminates in two amphorae at Munich (Figs. 76 and 78) and one in Castle Ashby, there enters into the old style varied, free and easy, broadly even laxly rendered, a peculiar severity and discipline. The three chief specimens, necked amphorae with the continuous scene preferred by the East, are more defined and elastic in shape, more finished in shape and colour, more ornamental and elaborate in the rendering of the figures, than was the case with the earlier style. The conclusion which naturally suggests itself, that this new spirit came from the West and the Chalkidian-Attic region, is confirmed by the ornaments. Beside the Ionic looped and plaited bands, leaf and bud friezes, and the continuous tendrils (Fig. 76), come the double rays, the Western palmette and lotus system ; and when the painter scatters animals among the ornaments (Fig. 76), he follows old Ionic tradition, but the hare and the hedgehog with the ostrich riders of the Castle Ashby amphora are of Corinthian origin (Fig. 66). In the treatment of the figure, the meeting of Eastern vigour and Western severity makes as charming an effect as the genuinely Ionic and very decorative composition; the scene of a Munich amphora arranged round a centre (Fig. 77) with the cunning Hermes, who creeping up on

86

tip-toe steals away the fair cow Io from the sleeping giant Argos, and the picture of the Centaurs hunting on the reverse (Fig. 78) are full of ornamental vigour and at the same time full of fresh observation. The left hand of the giant shows a new study of nature compared with the old-fashioned right of Hermes and left of the front Centaur; in the giant the artist is struggling to represent the anatomy, and the mantle of Hermes plainly falls in layers, in contrast with the absence of folds in the chiton.

The new impetus, which even expressed itself in exportation to Italy, could not save the Klazomenian manufactory from the preponderance of its Attic rival; it is at the same time its end. Not that the East Ionic decorative tendencies formed a blind alley; the combination with western technique ensured its continued life. But Asia Minor, which at this time fell into the hands of the Persians, was not a suitable soil for continued production. Athens seized not only the exportation but the entire production. The arrival at Athens of East Ionic artists is reflected not merely in the names of the vase-painters. When on the jug of Kolchos and the Attic vases, typical Eastern principles of composition crop up, when Nikosthenes introduces an East Ionic shape of amphora (Fig. 104), when the red-figured technique coming into existence on Klazomenian sarcophagi conquers the Attic workshops, when on early red-figure kylikes the same decorative tendencies which prevailed in the East assert themselves, there can be no question of an extinction of East Ionic art, but only of a re-birth in Athens, and a baptism with Attic spirit.

About on a level with the Castle Ashby group is another East Ionic class, also only known through export to Italy, the ' Caeretan hydriae,' so-called from the place where they were mostly found (amphorae and kraters being also represented), which are usually attributed to South East

GREEK VASE-PAINTING

Ionia. The developed vase-shapes, the completed black figure technique, which has a wash under the white and uses incision freely even for outlines, and the decoration, which has got beyond the animal style, make their late origin certain, and the agreement with Ephesian sculpture of about 550 B.C., expressed in treatment of hair, converging mantle folds and the graded edges of the drapery, clinches the matter. When in spite of that these vases stick fast to the system of contrast in colour, that agrees with an expressed preference for gay decoration such as from the days of the Naukratis vases South East Ionia loved. The 'Caeretan' painter actually enhances this colour preference, in that he varies the colour of the male body from black to dark red, bright yellow and white and similarly alternates the colour of hair and clothes. He gives the same motley effect to the ornamentation, which shows plainly its descent from the old Rhodian in its broad lotus and palmette system, its rosettes, hook-crosses, and spiral-crosses ornamenting the neck, and also reveals East Ionic freedom in natural myrtle branches and ivy-tendrils, in bucrania with festoons and in interspersed animals. The animal world too, with its fallow deer, lions, griffins, winged horses, and winged bulls, is characteristic of the East and the neighbourhood of Asia. These animals have long ceased to play their heraldic part, though on the reverse of the vase two may face each other in symmetrical correspondence ; they are rather by choice included in hunting scenes. The traditional tendency finds a refuge, if anywhere, in the figure scenes. In heraldic scenes of battle, in the horse-taming ' runner with bent knee,' in Satyr and Nymph running to meet each other, it asserts itself : but the living interest makes one forget the ornamental scheme. Lively drastic description is the strong point of the 'Caeretan' painter. His broadly treated scenes of hunting, fighting, and wrestling, the fine delineations of Satyr life, of the Heraklean legend, of Hermes and his theft of the kine, of the drunk and lame Hephaistos, of Europa carried by the bull over the sea, leave nothing to be desired in the way of original invention, healthy vigour, and naive vividness, and in their aversion to the typical and abstract they are diametrically opposed to Attic painting. The stocky, strong man Herakles with the curly hair who dispatches the inhospitable Pharaoh, Busiris, and his cowardly throng (Fig. 79), or who with the hound of hell frightens the Argive king into a wine jar (Fig. 81), are cabinet pictures of vigorous humour. The local colouring is also unmistakeable. The altar with volute profiles is an East Ionic architectural shape, the knowledge of the Egyptian and black races, of Egyptian priestly dress, of monkeys, can only have been obtained in Africa; the origin of the Busiris legend is only conceivable in the neighbourhood of the kingdom of the Pharaohs. Thus though the Caeretan vases found a local continuation in Etruria, because of this local colouring one cannot imagine them made by Ionian colonists in Caere.

On the other hand one may assume origin on Etruscan soil for another class of East Ionic style, only known from Etruria, called ' Pontic,' as having been wrongly localized on the Black Sea. The Asiatic-Ionian origin of the style is based on the vase shapes as on the choice, technique, types and application of the ornamental and animal decoration; and also the figures, the lines of Tritons and Nereids, riders and Scythians, heralds and Centaurs, and the legendary scenes, which are often under ornamental influence (Figs. 82 and 83) in execution and application, point to the same source. The 'Pontic' painters actually enrich our knowledge of East Ionic decorative motives by a series of combined lotus, palmettes, volutes, maeanders, by net patterns, leaf-friezes, etc., by a plentiful selection of animals, which

89

includes the marine Centaur, with the Asiatic man-bull, and is fond of lines of guinea-fowls. But on the whole the class is very provincial and cannot be regarded as a clear source of evidence. It is questionable, whether obstinate persistence in stripe decoration, only reluctantly giving way to the picture field, would have been possible in the mother-country well on in the 6th century. The style is visibly departing further from its Greek starting point. Vases which represent Lanuvian Juno (B.M. Cat. II. p. 66) or Etruscan winged demons, show in subject what the style of itself betrays.

Two classes with scanty decoration, fixed as East Greek by many finds, can only be named for completeness sake ; one, the 'Bucchero' ware long known in Etruria, which perhaps originated in Aeolis and which owes its black lustre not to glaze colour but to impregnation with charcoal and to polishing; the other, the ware with a great extension in South Asia Minor and Italy, either unadorned, or only decorated with stripes, which give important conclusions as to the development of vase-shapes.

The East Greek manner took the place of the Corinthian in Italy at the beginning of the 7th century. This revolution is less connected with importation than with the immigration of Ionic artists. But even the new current is more and more open to the influence of the ever-spreading Attic importation, which in the East and West not merely captures the market but also forces production under its spell.

Before we pass to this victorious fabric, we must once more return to Peloponnesus, to a fabric standing in isolation and of marked peculiarity, the Spartan. Excavations at Sparta show the transition to the black-figured style, such as took place elsewhere about the end of the 7th century. Corinth seems to have set the example for this transition ;

at all events Corinthian elements, *e.g.* riders with birds for space-filling in the black-figured style give this indication, though the conservative retention of the white slip and the inconsistent rendering of the male eye clearly distinguish it from Corinthian. It becomes really tangible to us at the period, when exportation properly begins, at a time which already puts a black wash under imposed white and with the shapes takes us further along into the 6th century. The ware for exportation, which spread far over the mainland to Naukratis and Samos as well as to Etruria, has given us only a few big vases, finely decorative works, which are very conservative in their adornment. The earliest of them is a Paris ' lebes ' with heraldically arranged animal-frieze and a frieze of figures above it, in which pot-bellied topers are placed between the Troilos story and a Centaur battle ; two volute kraters and two hydriae, by their shapes, cannot be much later. Broad tongues adorn shoulder and foot, the rays are doubled, to Geometric zig-zag and hooked bands are added upright arched friezes of lotus and pomegranate, continuous branches, and the lotus and palmette pattern ; the animal friezes have types of their own and do not avoid the processional order not ordinarily favoured in the West. Even the larger vases found in actual Spartan sanctuaries are almost entirely decorative and show little of the figure painting coming in so vigorously in other manufactories.

A compensation for this is offered by the number of kylikes preserved, which in the 6th century, as in East Ionia, Corinth and Athens, so also in Sparta, gradually pass into the high-stemmed shape with offset rim (Fig. 80). The outsides of these kylikes are adorned only in a few earlier specimens with antithetic or processional animal friezes, otherwise only with the simple or net-like pomegranate pattern, with lotus leaves and rays ; from the handles proceed palmettes on their sides. The figures are entirely confined to the interior, which much more commonly than in other manufactories, rises out of pure ornamentation or animal decoration to free scenic representations. To be sure this is often at the expense of the decorative effect. Most scenes are anything but composed with a view to a round space, and the segments under the line which marks the level of the ground, often very clumsily filled with plant and animal ornamentation, the rosettes, filling flowers, and birds dispersed without meaning about the scene, are always clumsy old-fashioned compromises between representation and space-filling. The stock of figures, with which the painter decorates his interiors, usually more or less at random, is even in its rendering helpless and antiquated; to make up it preserves its independence and ease, its primitive solidity; the strong warriors, riders and hunters, the men carousing with women, the musicians and drinkers, the girls bathing in the river, are in subject and execution truly Spartan. Beside the pictures from daily life comes mythology with pot-bellied dancers, who have not yet, so far as we know, been superseded by Ionic Satyrs, with Erotes crowning riders and drinkers, and various legendary scenes.

None of these kylix-pictures breathes the Spartan spirit, the spirit of the lyric poetry of Sparta, so well as the Berlin vase with the carrying home of fallen warriors, which is perhaps taken over from a continuous frieze without any attempt to fit it into the circular field; but even in this shape has the effect upon us of a funeral march of Kallinos or Tyrtaios (Fig. 84). But in humorous descriptiveness the Arkesilas vase (Fig. 85) takes the palm. It is a genre scene, but not this time from the life of a Spartan citizen, but a travel reminiscence of a painter, who once in African Cyrene looked on, while the silphion was weighed under the stern eye of Arkesilas, and stowed in the hold of a sailing ship to be exported. The monkey too, which the painter puts on the yard, he became acquainted with in Africa ; the birds are not meaningless but fly round the ship ; only the lizard is an external addition, and we already know it to be Corinthian. The life-like picture, which before the decisive excavations in Sparta was regarded as chief proof of Cyrenaic origin for this pottery, confirms the result of digging in the shape of the chair legs, which agree with Spartan reliefs, and in the inscription, only possible in Sparta. There is an approximate date given too ; for the king, whose portrait we have, reigned about the middle of the 6th century. With this it agrees that his mantle is divided into black and red stripes, which, as we saw in the Phineus kylix, comes before the rendering of folds.

This conservative style does not show the same keenness as its contemporaries in rendering folds and developing the knowledge of anatomy ; nor is the need felt for a long time of freeing the field from filling ornaments or the base segment from animal decoration. The group of vases which belongs to the second half of the century is especially marked by the return of the white slip and of polychromy in the ornamentation. It is only late that the Spartan painters turn to the rendering of folds and richer body details, really only in a time of decadence, which diminishes the foot, no longer colours the ornament, and often avoids the base-segment. The occasional use of pale red figures painted on a black ground with incised details can only be explained as a provincial imitation of Attic red-figured technique, with the superiority of which Sparta cannot even remotely compete. Similar vases without any figures show the last output of the fabric.

The only fabric in which the black-figured style completed its life and exhausted its possibilities, the only one which shows its living force through the archaic and classic periods, is the Attic. Even at the end of the 7th century it begins to vie with others. We already saw that Vurvá vases were exported to East Ionia ; the Gorgon lebes of the Louvre comes from Italy. Etruria now becomes the chief place where Attic and indeed all black-figured vases are found. The fact that ware made to be exported to Etruria first gave us the knowledge of Greek vase-painting, led enquiries on false tracks for a long time in localizing the fabrics, and even to-day the word 'vases' reminds us of the decisive finds on Italian soil.

The Attic manufactory is, as we saw, proved not only by the alphabet of their inscriptions but also by continuous finds in Attica itself. To be sure, the inequality of production in technique and style obtrudes itself on us here more than elsewhere, and makes us take fabric in a wider sense, as a complex of workshops, which turn out at the same time good and rubbishy ware, traditional and progressive painting, vases with light or dark-red clay. The Boeotian workshops, without doing them injustice, we may class with Attic workshops of the second class ; in the 6th century, in so far as they do not go on turning out their old bird kylikes (p. 52), they are only provincial offshoots of Attic industrial art. The same is the case with Eretria.

The inequality of Attic ware has yet other reasons. More than other fabrics the Attic adopted foreign influences. Athens' central position between Corinth, Chalkis and the Cyclades, its relations to East Ionia, led to a penetration of old Attic art traditions with other elements and to the formation of a new style : the rise of trade and industry enticed alien painters to settle at Athens, since foreign fabrics had more and more to give in to Athenian superiority. Thus it is that Corinthian, Chalkidian, ' Phineus,' East Ionic, occasionally even Spartan fabrics

94

are reflected in the Attic pottery.   These reflections give a very varied air to Attic pottery, but on the other hand help to a dating of its separate phases.   After a period of Corinthian influence follows one with a strong Chalkidian element, in the eye-kylikes the pattern of 'Phineus' ware is at work, while relations to East Ionic art run along side by side.

The group, which one is inclined to make parallel with the red-clay Corinthian, may be named the 'Sophilos' group from the fragments of a 'lebes' found on the Acropolis (Fig. 86).   In contrast with its immediate predecessor the Sophilos vase vies in motley effect with Corinthian ware. Ornament is richly painted ; himatia and borders are picked out in colour, women and linen chitons have a white filling ; in the red of the male face and the varied colouring of the horses the system of contrasted colours is as plainly exhibited as in the red colouring of the male breast or of the whole male body on other contemporary vases.   The marriage of Peleus and Thetis is the subject, in a type repeated on the François vase (Fig. 90), which we see developed on Corinthian kraters, probably under the influence of the chest of Kypselos.   Who introduced into the scene the Muse in front view playing on the syrinx, cannot be stated ; the lower part of the body in profile is in marked contrast with this bold front view ; that it is of ornamental origin, perhaps from a double Siren, might be suggested without its being too venturesome.

The frieze is framed between a broad lotus and palmette pattern and a stripe with large animals.   Whether the filling ornament has been omitted from the animal as well as from the figured frieze, in which nothing but the big lettering reminds us of the old requirement of filling the space, cannot be ascertained from this specimen ; a second vase of the same painter shows between the animals, which still suggest the Vurvá style, isolated large rosettes, and other vases of

95

this group make a palmette flower or bud with stalk project into the field. These isolated echoes of the old filling ornamentation, influenced by the East like the gradually appearing friezes of buds and leaves (p. 83) disappear about the middle of the century; but the animal friezes themselves live on longer.

This survival of old decorative tendencies in a new shape appears still more plainly in other vases of the "Sophilos" period. The amphorae, which leave a " metope " unpainted to carry their figures or make the figure field continuous, when they do not cover the whole body with stripes, have like the Klazomenian on the neck a head, a lotus and palmette cross, or a circle between zig-zags (the amphora which Dionysos is dragging on the François vase is of this type), and prefer still to decorate their stripes and fields with heraldically arranged animals. The Ionic liberties too, the meaningless compositions, are not infrequent, just as beside many Corinthian echoes in the friezes of animals and riders, Ionic patterns often assert themselves in the drawing and colouring of the animals, and in the shape and decoration of the vases. The kraters and hydriae which are parallel with the Corinthian, give the same impression. Of the smaller vases we may select two hasty compositions, which cannot compare with the fine work of Sophilos, but in their way help to enlarge our idea of the period. The Munich tripod-vase (Fig. 87) in the stripe on the rim shows alongside of the old animal composition two wrestlers of the Corinthian scheme and a horse race from the same source, the succession of which is interrupted by a fallen horse just as the animal friezes of contemporary vases contain fighting animal groups; and a kantharos of Boeotian manufacture and shape (Fig. 88) over the animal frieze introduces the wild dancers, who as at Corinth, Chalkis and in East Ionia prepare the way for the Satyrs.

THE BLACK-FIGURED STYLE

Just as we followed the process in late Corinthian and Chalkidian workmanship, so in Athens the broad, massive archaic black-figured style in the shape of the vase and the rendering of the figures passes into more and more elegant compression and precision ; Sophilos is followed by Klitias. The Florence vase ' made ' by the potter Ergotimos, ' painted ' by Klitias and named after its finder François (Figs. 89 and 90), even in the boldly rising outline of the body shows the spirit of a new age, and goes beyond the round-bellied shape of the Gorgon ' lebes ' as much as the late Corinthian kraters surpass the Eurytios vase (Fig. 64). Ergotimos holds the mean between the old round-bellied vase shapes and the more elegant ones of the Chalkidian best period (p. 77), just as Klitias does between the figured style of Sophilos and that of Amasis (p. 105) ; and as Ergotimos does his best in delicately moulding the shape and gives the vase a showy appearance with his elongated handle volutes, so in the figured decoration covering the whole surface and in the incredibly delicate execution of all details Klitias presents a refinement of the black-figured style which in its way cannot be surpassed. Potter and painter here take a step, which secures for Attic pottery the paramount position for all time.

The treatment of the procession of the Olympians in honour of the newly-wedded sea-goddess on the principal frieze is particularly rich. We have seen that Klitias here utilized an old type. The representative solemnity required by the subject gives an archaic stamp to this frieze ; in particular the richly adorned festal clothes with patterns that it almost requires a microscope to see, which bear witness to uncanny patience and accuracy on the part of the painter, heighten the stiffly venerable impression. But when compared with Sophilos, Klitias shows a considerable advance in the rendering of nature.

97

For that we must not lay stress on the head of Dionysos in front view, for the god's mask-like appearance passed from cult into vase-painting; but we may point to the diminished heaviness of the figures, the smaller size of the eye, the division of the himatia into stripes, which here and there converge like folds, and the reduction in size of the inscriptions. The other friezes exhibit Klitias as a master of the delineation of life and movement : the arrival of the ship of Theseus at Delos (Fig. 89), the hunt of Meleager, the battle with the Centaurs, the chariot-race, the return of Hephaistos, the adventure of Troilos, and the delightful frieze on the foot with the battle of dwarfs and cranes ; even the heraldic animal frieze is seized by the same liveliness, for between the heraldic sphinxes and griffins the animals, now treated in quite an elegant and concise way, are attacking each other. How much of these scenes is due to the inventiveness of Klitias and his direct observation of nature cannot be made out. He has not got the rough freshness and naturalism of the Ionic painters, but instead a marked feeling for clear and speaking types ; and generally speaking, discipline and the gift of abstraction seem to have been more characteristic of the Athenians than of the Ionians, who set more carelessly to work. Perhaps Klitias got from eastern masters the interruption of the heraldry in the animal frieze by fighting groups ; and at any rate the Satyrs who accompany the drunken Hephaistos come from the East into Attic pottery.

In the technique of the figures, the old style is worthily putting forth its last efforts ; the white is still put direct on the clay, the man's face is coloured red, black horse alternates with white. But with the perfection of the clay and the black used in painting, and the minute detail of incised lines, a new feeling for colour is brought in, which leads away from the old motley effect; the masters of the

François vase themselves in their later works go over to the new system, which paints a ground for the white and gives up red in the male body, a system which, perhaps, other less thorough artists had already set going.

The chariot-race for a prize on the neck of the François vase introduces us to an old and popular contest, which according to tradition Pisistratus replaced by other games, when in 566 B.C. he reformed the Panathenaea. At the same time he must have erected a new image of Athena on the Acropolis, which, in opposition to the old conception, (p. 66) still followed by the François vase, represented the goddess in full armour. For on the prize vases, which were given to the victors full of precious oil and labelled ' one of the prizes from the city of Athens ' ($\tau\hat{\omega}\nu$ 'A$\theta\acute{\eta}\nu\eta\theta\epsilon\nu$ $\ddot{\alpha}\theta\lambda\omega\nu$), Athena always appears as a fighting warrior, just as the poet Stesichoros and paintings of the time of Sophilos had made her leap from the head of Zeus. The oldest of these Panathenaic amphorae (an idea of their shape is given by Fig. 101, a later specimen of about 520 B.C.) shows on the obverse the new type of Athena in the making, and on the reverse the chariot-race which was now becoming infrequent. Since this vase adheres closely to the Sophilos group in style and especially in the animal decoration of the neck, but on the other hand already has a painted ground for white, it will not be possible to move the François vase and the transition to the later technique away from the sixties of the 6th century.

The group of kraters, lebetes, hydriae, amphorae and other vases, which immediately adheres to the François vase, usually, in so far as it is not interrupted by marked individualities, is described by the antiquated name 'Tyrrhenian,' derived from the finds in Etruria. The conservative and often mechanical character of these vases does not conceal the progressive elements. The vases assume the more slender egg-shaped form known to us from Chalkis, the old neck ornament of the amphorae (p. 96) is replaced by lotus and palmette. White colour is regularly placed on black ground; Herakles is often equipped with the lion's skin; Athena with at any rate helmet and spear; in place of the old-fashioned burlesque dancers and naked women come Satyrs and Maenads. But of improvements in observation of nature this second-class group has hardly any to show. It lives on the achievements of great masters, on Corinthian traditions, and eastern influences. The frieze amphorae, which continue alongside of the amphorae with picture field, vie with the François vase in the accumulation of figured friezes; only in the lower stripe they economize in figure scenes by using lines of lotus and palmettes and animals. Thus their general appearance is still very like the Vurvá vases, the Gorgon lebes and many vases of the Sophilos period. The traditions of the 7th century end in this mechanical group; the great masters of the second third of the century bring, perhaps from Chalkis, new vase types and new kinds of decoration.

The transition may first be followed in the Kylix, which happily can be traced in its development by many signed specimens. The firm of Ergotimos produces a cup with knobbed handles and no set-off for the rim, the interior picture of which is framed by tongue pattern, thus a kylix of the type known to us from Corinth and Chalkis; on the outside the Satyr is still loosely connected with drinkers of the old type, and has thus not yet been associated with Dionysos and the Maenads. This type of kylix shews marked Chalkidian influence, especially in later specimens like that of Boston (Fig. 92), on which Circe (painted white over black) hands to the companions of Odysseus the fatal potion and so brings about her own abrupt end. Series of branches and buds, probably also the dog in front view (p 81) and much in the style of the figures come from the neighbouring fabric. This Chalkidian influence is to be traced on a second type of kylix belonging to this period, that with off-set rim, (not the one in Circe's hand), which for a time carelessly draws its figures over the junction, but finally makes a clean cut between handle frieze and rim ornament : the rim is *e.g.* decorated with a branch or painted black, the handle frieze bears figures or the artist's signature in neat letters between the palmettes proceeding from the handles. The masters of the François vase themselves took this step forward ; in Naukratis and the interior of Asia Minor signed specimens have been found, speaking documents of the popularity of the fine Attic ware in the East, which help to explain the alteration of the Ionic style (p. 86).

The workshop of Ergotimos passed to his son Eucheiros (B.M. Cat. ii., p. 221), who, like the sons of Nearchos, Ergoteles and Tleson (B.M. Cat. ii., p. 222) is found among the so-called ' little masters,' the makers of dedicated high-stemmed cups, who, with special pride, and probably also for decorative reasons, put their names on their products. More than twenty makers' names, among them those of Exekias, Pamphaios, Charitaios, Hischylos, and Nikosthenes, have been handed down to us on these vases, an important piece of evidence for the vigour of Attic production in the generation after Klitias and Ergotimos. These masters preserve the division between handle and rim stripes, even when the rim is not marked off from the body. As with Klitias, the handle stripe bears the master's inscription or a drinking motto ; in this case the representation, consisting of neat miniature figures or a female head drawn in fine outline, moves into the upper stripe (Fig. 91). Side by side with that, the painting of the rim black and decoration of the handle stripe with figures are very common. In the figures decorative tendencies, betokening intention rather than convention, assert themselves. The interior picture often consists of the Gorgon's mask, or a figure to fill the space to fit the circle; the outside often bears meaningless compositions (heraldic animals, winged creatures, runners, riders, men wrapped in cloaks), out of which develop scenes of hunting and pursuit, chariot-races, and cock-fights; but also mythological scenes and vigorous battle pictures with many figures occur. When such scenes are still flanked by heraldic animals, in this case primitive traditions are consciously retained.

On the Munich kylix (Fig. 91) the painter in the inscription praises the beauty of Kalistanthe. More commonly fair boys are praised, a practice which continues on vases for a century, the explanation being supplied by the erotic scenes represented from the later time of Klitias. Those celebrated are seldom to be regarded as the favourites of the vase-painters themselves, but generally sons of the best society, for whom there was a furore. This worship of beauty is of use to the historian, for many of the *Kaloi* are great persons with established dates, and anyhow the common love-name puts all vases which bear it into a short period of time; for the bloom of beauty lasts not more than a decade.

If the kylikes of the 'little masters' last to the beginning of the red-figured style (p. 109), the eye-cups go a good bit beyond this limit. The type must have been brought to Athens from the 'Phineus' manufactory (p. 80) in the later period of the 'little masters'; and perhaps the Ionian Amasis, who has left a fine specimen with a figure holding a branch between the eyes, had much to do with this naturalization. Certainly the Attic artists never rival the swelling shapes and vigorous life of their prototypes. With this type the outside begins again to be treated as a decorative unit without division, an arrangement of which the red-figured style makes almost exclusive use. The interior is generally not more richly decorated than by the ' little masters.' When Exekias on one vase adorns the whole interior surface with a wonderful idyll, the giver of the vine in a sailing boat with dolphins leaping round him, this is quite an exception (Fig. 93) : that the ground is painted brick-red, is quite unique.

The names Ergotimos and Klitias, Exekias and Amasis, Charitaios, Pamphaios and Nikosthenes show that the manufacture of kylikes was by no means a separate speciality, and that it may be simply due to accident if certain firms producing larger vases do not recur among the ' little masters.'

The larger masterpieces naturally show the progress of the style much more plainly than the conservative Tyr-rhenian ware and the kylikes. We noticed above, that single specimens, which stand out markedly from the ordinary ware of the period, attach themselves to the François vase. The master of a fine lebes from the Acropolis showing Ionic influence, who occasionally still colours the male face red, probably emigrated from the East like his contemporaries Kolchos and Lydos. Like Klitias, the masters prefer to cover garments with rich patterns rather than to render folds : they relieve the monotony of white chitons by vertical strokes, and divide the surfaces of cloaks into stripes. This division does not yet attain any effect of depth. But when Nearchos, the father of two " little masters ' (pp. 101 and 112), divides the short male chiton also by wavy lines into black and red stripes, he has already in his mind the rendering of folds, and Kolchos grades the ends of cloaks with clear folds. This emancipation from the old superficiality, which in the period of the ' little masters ' leads to the emergence of the ' fold ' style in the

103

works of Amasis and Exekias, must now be exhibited in a selection of amphorae and hydriae in connection with the change of vase-shapes and decoration.

We begin with the big-bellied amphora, which at the end of the 7th century we saw reserve a square field and decorate it with horses' or women's heads, and which in the period of Sophilos begins to put an upper border of ornament on its figure-field, which is often adorned with animals. Fine specimens of the Klitias period, which banish the animal ornament into a lower frieze or give it up altogether, show an obvious change in shape, in that the handles, instead of standing off like ears, are drawn up perpendicularly, while the body of the vase is to some degree tightened. Vases like that of Taleides with the slaying of the Minotaur, or like the unsigned Iliupersis vase in Berlin (Fig. 94) with the gay alternate palmette pattern and the old heavy foot of the François vase, belong to this class. On both vases standing figures form an extension of an animated central group, but the Iliupersis master makes a better whole of his triptych than Taleides, who merely juxtaposes the heroes' conflict and the spectators : alongside of the furious Neoptolemos, who has already laid one Trojan low and is on the point of despatching the aged king and his grandson with one blow, Menelaos threatens his faithless wife, whom he has won back, while on the other side Priam's entreaties are supported by wife and daughter : a picture rich in content, of true archaic vividness and talkativeness, excellently drawn and composed. It is not only the way in which white is used that takes one beyond the François vase ; the rosette ornamentation of the garments is quite typical of the following period (Fig. 92) ; the wavy striping of the short chiton and the simple grading of the cloak reminds us of Nearchos and Kolchos, and whether Klitias could have characterized a dying man as well as our master is at least

104

questionable.

The current of Chalkidian influence, which sets in vigorously about this time, seizes also the body amphora. The arched foot becomes more plate-like, a clay-ring unites it with the end of the body, which is more taper; the Chalkidian wreath of buds (Fig. 71) for a time commonly takes the place of the palmette and lotus band, which becomes scantier and more monotonous, and as at Chalkis, a figure frieze (Fig. 95) may occupy this space. The type belongs to the earlier ' little master ' period. From Exekias, who was himself in his off-hours a ' little master,' comes a specimen in the Louvre with the praise of the fair Stesias, a youthful work of this worthy successor of Klitias, on which Chalkidian patterns are very finely worked out, without the slightest attempt at the rendering of folds.

The unsigned Würzburg amphora of Amasis (Fig. 95), like all the vases of this master peculiar in shape and of perfect technique, is more progressive and probably somewhat later than the Stesias amphora of Exekias: the cloak of Dionysos on the obverse is laid in three folds; on the reverse the shaggy satyrs, stylized in a quite un-Attic way, who to the sound of the flute are gathering, pressing, and distributing into jars the beloved gift of the god, show the same connection with the ' Phineus ' factory as the eye kylix (p. 102). The technical perfection and the fine decorative effect of Amasis' vases are only surpassed by a wonderful contemporary group, which is usually called the ' affected ' class, because it consciously sacrifices the living representation of the figure world to the ornamental general effect.

The over-elegant works of Exekias, the ' affected ' vases, the minute ' little master ' kylikes represent the last refinement of the silhouette style, its last trump-card. The future belonged not to the masters of the adorned surface, but to the delineators of the surface in movement. In the last phase of the body amphora prior to the red-figured style, in which the band-like handles and the narrower neck are drawn higher and the stiff palmette pattern becomes canonical, Exekias in his riper development passes over to rich rendering of folds; on the harmonious amphora in Rome, which no longer praises Stesias but Onetorides (Fig. 96) he exhibits in the cloaks of the players the last possibilities of his subtle technique with an almost incredible devotion to detail, but even these fine clothes have their edges overlapping, and on the reverse of the vase, besides foldless patterned clothes, appear cloaks richly animated with folds. The amphora must be of the same period as the eye kylix (Fig. 93); not only the feeling as a whole but the dark-red chitons in layers on the outside point to the late activity of the master.

The necked amphorae complete our idea of the two great masters. The old heavy shapes with the arched foot take up Chalkidian influences and go through the same processes of change, which we know from Chalkis. The old-fashioned decoration with animal stripes is retained by the Tyrrhenian vases, that with continuous pictorial field by the 'affected' group for a time, till the later Chalkidian type conquers the whole field (Fig. 69). Amasis seems not merely to have introduced it into Athens but also to have created the pretty variation with the flat shoulder with a rectangular turn and the wide handles running out below into tendrils: for these continuous tendrils are old property of his eastern home. The handle ornament separates off the pictures on the two sides and liberates the figures from the constraints of a frieze. The Paris amphora with Dionysos and the interesting group of embracing Maenads (Fig. 98) is closely connected with the Würzburg amphora (Fig. 95) not only by the double rays, which Amasis loves, by the grouping, which in the other vase is transferred without change to satyrs, by the beginning of himation folds, but also by many details of the very individual style. The aversion to white colour is interesting. On both vases the linen chiton of the god is left black; the Paris maenads are rendered in outline only: it is but seldom that the reaction against the old parti-coloured scheme goes so far. Parallels are provided by the Athena of Kolchos' jug and the girl-busts of the ' little masters ' (Fig. 91). Both the other amphorae of Amasis are more advanced. The shape of the vase is slimmer, the decoration simpler, the relation of figures to space freer. The bodies are no longer the thick-set broad-thighed type of the older style: the eye plays no longer so prominent a part. The short chiton is not merely laid in black and red layers but even provided with a quite naturally waving border: the artist thus far surpasses the standard of Exekias and even of early red-figured masters. He need not on that account be put very late, for the simple Ionic masters of the Caeretan hydriae, perhaps his countrymen, made this border before him. This Ionism is in favour of Amasis, who signs only as potter, having himself painted all his vases, and having played the pioneer not only in vase shapes and decoration but also in figure style. Exekias (in whose works the unity of the whole is often expressly emphasized by the inscription ' made and painted me ') does not attack the problem of folds so boldly. Even on the two fine necked amphorae, which praise the favourite of his later period, as a good Athenian he lays the drapery in neatly-ironed layers.

The slender Munich necked amphora (Fig. 97) goes still further beyond the Chalkidian models (Fig. 69). The neck ornament connects it with the late works of Exekias, the eye decoration with the kylix type of the same time, and even

the space-filling vine-tendrils, which perhaps Amasis introduced from the ' Phineus ' factory into Attic painting, are
a favourite motive in later times.   The satyr mask, like the
Dionysos mask, probably passed from cult into decorative
painting; if Klitias represents Dionysos, and Amasis the
satyr, with head in front view, the influence of these masks
is not to be mistaken.

We have not yet named the most productive amphora
painter.   Nikosthenes supplied some fine examples of the
method of Amasis, some of which like the Exekias lebes
(Fig. 99) on the body of the vase help the fine black colour to
exclusive possession ; besides a quantity of notably metallic
amphorae   with   band   handles,   the   production   of
which in quantities seems to be his speciality, though other
masters adopted and modified the shape (Fig. 104).   The
often very hasty and conservative decoration of these vases
cannot   come   from   one   painter.   Nikosthenes, of whom
almost   a   hundred   signed   vases   are   extant   (kraters,
' Amasis ' and ' Nikosthenes ' amphorae, ' little master '
kylikes, eye kylikes, neatly painted jugs with white ground,
and   red-figured vases) must have employed a series of
painters.   The only one who gives his name, Epiktetos, we
shall hear of later.

The hydria too, which often shows its use in pretty fountain scenes (Fig. 106), alters its form.   As in Chalkis (p. 76)
the egg-shaped type of the Klitias period, shown e.g. on the
Troilos frieze of the François vase, gradually gives way to
the later type with picture field and horizontal, separately
adorned shoulder.   Timagoras, a contemporary of Exekias,
still prefers a broad-bellied shape and does not form handle
and foot as elegantly as Pamphaios.   His Paris vase with
the later type of the contest with Triton (p. 67), on which
he still paints the monster's face red for colour contrast, is
very important for chronology by a declaration of love for

Andokides, a young colleague and later chief master of the early red-figured style. If Timagoras is the predecessor of Andokides, Pamphaios is his rival. His slim London hydria with the slightly bent up handles, on which the vine of Dionysos overgrows the whole picture, and the dark-red striping of the cloak assumes pure fold-character, falls into the red-figured period, which after the second third of the century begins to compete with the old technique, and to which Pamphaios himself opens his workshop. The new style did not abruptly drive out the old : from the time of its predominance perhaps more black-figured vases are preserved than from the preceding period. In the leading studios for a time both techniques were practised side by side, often by the same painters. The balance inclined quickly to the side of the style which painted the background and not the figure, and after the transitional time of Andokides and Pamphaios only inferior talents experiment in the old silhouette style. But though driven out of the leading position, this old style was still busy and productive at least to the beginning of the 5th century : especially necked amphorae and hydriae, which the new style did not zealously affect, keep the tradition.

At this later date the shapes become elongated, the lotus and palmette ornament loses colour, sweep and consistency. The hydriae bend their handles more steeply upwards : the row of palmettes enclosed by tendrils is preferred as framing ornament. The figures move more freely in the space, and are also more hastily drawn ; in particular the rendering of folds becomes regular. The red stripes, which are painted quite meaninglessly between the folds, no longer remind us that they once indicated sewed parts of garments ; white rosettes and red spots serve as surface patterns, a red stroke as border. On the fine hydria in Berlin (Fig. 100) probably of Euphronios' time, which, it is true, is quite unlike its class, the old round formation of the eye actually approximates to the natural oval.

The links with the red-figured style, especially common love names like Hipparchos, Pedieus, and Leagros, help us to date this style. Thus the circumscribed row of palmettes seems to appear in the early Leagros period (p. 114) ; the Berlin vase is thus moved to the end of the century, like a group of pelikai with charming genre scenes and a series of other vases of red-figured shape (p. 119).

In the new century the black-figured production gradually dies away. Apart from the Panathenaic amphorae (p. 99) and other vases, which for ritual reasons remain conservative, only trifling small ware keeps up the old style. The prize vases can be followed as votive offerings on the Acropolis, and in exported specimens down into the 4th century, where they are dated to the year by archons' names (one of 313 B.C. has been found) ; even in late times they do not give up the old type of Athena, but elongate it to agree with the slender proportions of the vase, and combine other later features with the old picture.

In Boeotia black-figured painting, alongside of primitive attempts to imitate Attic red-figured vases, continued as long in the burlesque parodies of myth of the so-called ' Kabirion ' vases ; black painting on a light ground is found in the early Hellenistic ' Hadra vases ' made at Alexandria, and similar late phenomena occur in various localities. These late black-figured vases show real progress in nothing but the development of a loose freely moving vegetable ornamentation : but this progress depended on pure brush-technique, not on the old incised style.

CHAPTER V.

THE RED-FIGURED STYLE IN THE ARCHAIC PERIOD

HOW the sudden change of technique took place, how the idea suggested itself, that instead of painting silhouettes on the ground of the clay, figures drawn in outline should be left free to contrast with the black background, is not yet explained. The inversion of the colour system is not new. From Ionic, Corinthian, Attic, and Boeotian workshops we know of light painting on a dark ground, and a plate from Thera has light figures in added paint and a black background. But this is entirely different from the red-figured style, which uses the ground of the clay for its figures. Only late Klazomenian sarcophagi can be regarded as its earlier stages, and it is quite possible that the new technique was naturalized in Athens by East Ionic painters.

At any rate the idea fell on fruitful soil. The archaic mixture of colour was long worn out, the simplification of colour-effect, by increasing limitation to the two values, clay and glaze, was in full swing, and the effect of big glazed surfaces had been tried in the body-amphorae and in vessels completely covered with black colour (p. 108). But more than all else the revolution in figure-drawing which was now setting in strong in the great art was striving for expression in vase painting. A successor of the Athenian Eumares, Kimon of Kleonai, according to Pliny, invented oblique views and foreshortening, rescued the body from archaic stiffness, furnished limbs with joints, for the first

111

time rendered veins, and represented folds and swellings of drapery ; he must belong to the last third of the century ; for his predecessor is father of the sculptor Antenor, who worked, it is true, for the old potter Nearchos (p. 103) but also for the young Athenian Republic (510 B.C.) Though Pliny, after the fashion of ancient historians, is too fond of asserting ' inventions,' this much is clear, that after Eumares there was a breach with tradition in Athenian painting, and that here, for the first time in the history of the world, bonds were once for all burst, which hitherto had hardly been touched. Naturally the vase-painters could not be left behind ; but since the old silhouette incised style was quite unsuited for the new liberties of drawing, but on the other hand outline drawing on light ground ran counter to the decorative purposes of the vases which used silhouettes, the idea of inverting the colour-scheme must have been received with enthusiasm among the vase-painters.

The new invention unites the enhanced freedom of movement of the draughtsman with a decorative effect which is not inferior to that of the old style. The warm red inner surface of the figures, which the painter can animate by the brilliant sweeping ' relief lines,' splendidly contrasts with the wonderful black lustre of the ground. The new style too is a silhouette style, and uses the ornamental effect of the figures. But it contains quite different possibilities, and of itself moves away from the types of the old style and towards an individual treatment of the figures. The contrast between the black silhouette of the man and the white-filled figure of the woman falls away, also the circular shape of the man's eye connected with the incised style, the gay dresses, and much besides. The red-figured style enters into the characteristic working out of the human body and its parts, the study of drapery folds and the rendering of movement in a living way. But growing naturalism is in true Greek fashion contemporaneous with adherence to types; formulæ once invented are retained and repeated by different masters, until new discoveries by bolder spirits outdo them and put them in the shade. In the archaic red-figured style this vigorous struggle between formula and bold observation of nature offers an exciting spectacle. Step by step the ground is won from the archaic style, till after a struggle of about fifty years, about the time of the Persian wars, a free rendering of nature is attained, which then lays the foundation for the formation of a new and higher series of types, for the style of Polygnotos and Phidias.

This period may be regarded as the culminating point of vase-painting altogether, if emphasis is laid on the intensity of the line, and on the intimate relation between artist and technique. In it artistic craft had its greatest triumphs and created the most perfect synthesis between ornamental types and delightful naturalism. Potters and painters were never again so conscious of their performances as in this period, never again felt themselves so much as rival individualities. Certainly the old black-figured masters, Timonidas, Klitias, Exekias and Amasis, cannot be denied personal expression. But the red-figured conquerors of nature, each of whom in his own way breaks through the old system of type, produce a far more differentiated effect. It is also a result of the fresh current, which now enters vase-painting, that we can more than ever follow the development of these individualities. The signatures, which are preserved in such number from no other period, give an insight, not merely into the manifold production, but also into the growth of personalities and their struggle for ever new possibilities.

Among the signatures we must distinguish between potters and painters. We must never assume that the

' maker ' is responsible for the adornment of his vases ; it looks rather as if the painters had lived pretty independently and been employed first by one and then by another proprietor of a workshop. What it means, that now the potter signs, now the painter, sometimes both together, and that many strong personalities do not sign at all, cannot be made out in the present state of our knowledge.

The love-names help to fix the chronology of the vases still more than in the black-figured style. We saw that Andokides was *kalos*, when Timagoras' workshop was in full swing. When he is a full-blown painter, the ' Epiktetan ' kylikes and an Oxford plate celebrate the youths Stesagoras, Hipparchos and Miltiades. If Miltiades is the victor of Marathon, Stesagoras his brother, and Hipparchos the archon of 496 B.C., their ephebic years and these vases must be fixed about 520 B.C. Memnon's youth must fall about the same time ; for one of the many kylikes with his name, like a lekythos signed by Gales, shows the bard Anakreon, who was entertained by the Pisistratidae, 522-514 B.C. The painters Phintias and Euthymides praise the youth Megakles ; now on a votive pinax from the Acropolis this name was replaced later by another, and it is a plausible guess to connect this erasure with the banishment of a Megakles in 486 B.C., who about twenty-five years before might have deserved these praises. The youthful beauty of Leagros is in the time of the vase-painter Euphronios, and anyhow earlier than the destruction of Miletos, in which a Leagros vase was shattered : the Leagros who fell in battle as Strategos 465 B.C., must have been an ephebus in the last decade of the 6th century. His son Glaukon, who was Strategos in 440 B.C., dates the vases which celebrate him with his father's name a generation later, so about 470 B.C. The only established fact from finds does not contradict the ' Leagros ' chronology ; in the tumulus of

114

Marathon (490 B.C.) the latest offering was a sherd of the kylix type with simple maeander (c.p. Fig. 115) which appears in the later 'Leagros' period. The Acropolis finds, which are prior to the Persian conflagration (480 B.C.), have not yet been sorted and sifted.

According to this chronology the red-figured style must have made its entry into Athens about fifty years before the Persian War, with which it is customary to close the archaic period of Greek art, *i.e.*, about 530 B.C.

We saw above, that the workshops of Pamphaios and Nikosthenes open their doors to it : neither master breaks abruptly with the old style, which often asserts itself together with the new on the same vase. This contrast of the two styles is made clear by no one more obviously than the potter Andokides on his fine amphorae, which are directly in line of succession with Exekias ; never is the essence of both styles so plain as when on such a vase the same subject is treated by the same painter's hand in the old and in the new technique. The unsigned, but certainly Andokidean Munich amphora (Fig. 103) is not one of these instances in spite of the similarity of the subject ; its black-figured Herakles scene is certainly by a different hand from its red-figured, in which the same delicate and original artist as on most of the signed works (the 'Andokides' painter) expresses himself. If this painter is identical with the potter, Andokides was not merely in shape and decoration of his vases but also as draughtsman a pupil and successor of Exekias. He has inherited the feeling for elegant detailed drawing and for richly ornamented garments. In the Herakles scene we see the same joy in a harmonious picture as in the sea-voyage of Exekias (Fig. 93) and the game of draughts (Fig. 96), which he actually copied ; and the same intense absorption in the subject makes all other works of Andokides charming. In much the drawing reminds us of the teacher, particularly the flat layers of drapery, which already resolve the chitons into rich folds and end in the border more naturally, but do not attain the life-like waving of the late works of Amasis. The filling of the space with vine branches also is more in accord with the old technique than the new. But the more advanced pupil is shown not merely by the renewed study of the body, which appears in the drawing of hand and foot, in pointed elbow and knee, and in Herakles' leg shown through the drapery, but also by the more compact composition and the individual treatment of the heads.

The entirely red-figured vases by Andokides are not necessarily older than the black-figured: the latest vase signed by him (in Madrid) still combines both techniques. It must have been decorated by a third artist less archaic in feeling, who also worked for the potter firm of Menon. The Menon painter adds to the Andokidean framing patterns the row of circumscribed palmettes, though not yet in their final shape, and approximates in style to the young Euphronios and his rival Euthymides. The ornament of the Madrid vase does not seem to have been devised as border pattern. It must be derived from the tendril-composition, which on red-figured vases takes the place of the Amasis ornament (Fig. 98) and is in great favour as handle-ornament for kylikes. On the fine amphora in Paris, which the transitional master Pamphaios made after the patterns of Nikosthenes, and Oltos probably painted with scenes of hetairai and satyrs (Fig. 104), it appears as handle decoration together with an equally novel calyx and leaf ornament, which adorns the shoulder. The free decorative method of composition, which can be traced back through Amasis (p. 105) and Klazomenai to the Fikellura style (p. 61) is exactly in the manner of the red-figured style, which not only shakes off the frieze constraint but even the pictorial field : on the amphora, which the same painter executed for the potter Euxitheos, he discards the old frame, which now only separates black from black, and his example is followed sooner or later by other artists.

It is true that the painter Euthymides, the contemporary of the young Euphronios and gifted continuer of Andokides' body amphorae, keeps the frame on his vases, which are now purely red-figured. But he not only helps the later palmette ornament to triumph over the old bands of zig-zags and buds (Fig. 105) but enhances the unity of effect by beginning to leave the ornament in the colour of the clay and to shape it in red-figured manner, as was the case straight away with the handle decoration (Fig. 104). Almost as a rule he puts in his field three standing figures of large dimensions, in which he demonstrates to the eye his progress in observation of nature. Under the garments bodies begin to move, and their anatomy male and female is studied by the artists of this period with tireless zeal.

The fruits of this study appear on the Munich Priam vase (Fig. 105), in the drawing of hands, in the differentiated pose of the legs, in the bold front view of the foot, still more on the reverse in the bendings and turnings of three naked drunken men with full indication of muscles. Certainly the limitations of his eye for perspective appear, when the further from sight of the two chest muscles comes under the nearer one, when the woman's breast is turned outwards, when the transition of the breast seen in front view to the legs in profile is not made clear, and the head of the man walking to the right and looking round in archaic fashion is still turned in profile to the left ; the artist, it is true, breaks through the old scheme of the figure in one place, but his avoidance of lines shewing depth is so strong that he prefers to put those parts of the body, of whose front and back he is conscious, simply one beside the other. But it is

117

J

just the contrast between the bold attempt at progress on the painter's part and the perspective constraint, the feeling of conflict, if you like, that gives their charm to the vase-paintings of this period.

Though the bodies are no longer as previously packed into the garments, and drapery is rather subordinate to the treatment of the body, studies in drapery also have been very fruitful. The contrast between the heavy woollen himation, and the more delicate crinkles of the linen chiton is plainly marked. The depths of the folds in the cloak, according as they are close together or more freely distributed, are given in gradation by thicker or thinner lines of colour; the chiton folds join in separate masses and run out in the expressive so-called swallow-tail borders, which divide the outline of the drapery much more rhythmically than the layered borders of the 'Andokides' painter.

Chalkidian painters had already rendered scenes of arming. But those of Euthymides mark a great psychological advance. The paternal anxiety of the bald-pated old man and the nervousness of the mother's pet making his first début are finely expressed. The feeling for everyday life, in an age which suddenly recognized in common things a world of artistic problems, was keener than ever. What cared Euthymides about his subject "Hector's departure"? He drew a scene from his neighbour's door and added heroic names.

His best work the master left unsigned, the Munich amphora, on which Theseus under protest from Helen (note the thumb) with gay impudence carries off Korone (Fig. 107). The head of the ravisher, which gets its increased liveliness not merely from the shifting of the pupil from the centre inwards, may serve as example of the newly-conquered possibilities of expression, and the extract from the picture may give an idea of the charm of archaic art.

118

RED-FIGURED STYLE—ARCHAIC PERIOD

The Bonn hydria of Euthymides with the praise of Megakles shows a quite new type of vase; in contrast to the offset black-figured shape, it unites neck and body in an elegant curve, so that the old-fashioned division of the decoration into two or three parts disappears. The same fair youth is praised by his gifted colleague Phintias, whom we see from his beginnings in the workshop of Deiniades expanding more and more brilliantly, on a London hydria of the old shape; but the gracefully moving boys, who in the picture while drawing water are addressed by an older man, already carry water-pots of both types in their hands, and Phintias himself occasionally adopted the later shape; as does the painter Hypsis with the pretty well-house scene (Fig. 106), on which again both vase-shapes are represented; for the girl, who is just putting the cushion on her head, has placed a pitcher of the old type under the lion's head spout from which the water is pouring, while her companion is lifting a hydria of the new shape already well-filled from the satyr's mouth. The intensive study of the female form is seen in Oltos' picture of a hetaira (Fig. 104) and in many other vase-paintings of the period, and even when they represent girls clothed, the painters are unwilling to sacrifice their newly-won knowledge to external probability, and even under the drapery help the charm of the body outline to assert itself, as Hypsis does on his well-scene (Fig. 106).

Like the Bonn hydria, the works of Euthymides witness to the emergence of new vase-types, the Turin psykter and the unsigned Vienna pelike. An idea may be obtained of the psykter (which is regarded as a cooling vessel) by the later example in Rome (Fig. 104) in which the narrower cylindrical lower part is however missing. The pelike is a kind of small wineskin-shaped amphora. Even the transitional artist Pamphaios gave Oltos a stamnos (cp. Fig. 146)

119

to paint, and the early red-figured artist Smikros painted one. The calyx-krater, a kind of enlarged cup with low-set handles, seems to appear in the Leagros period (Fig. 113). The remarkable vases in the shape of a head (Figs. 101, 109) in a smaller form served for the reception of unguents and oil even in Protocorinthian and early Ionic styles, but seem only at this time to become popular as bumpers in the service of the drinker, and the pretty heads of negroes and girls with the love-names Epilykos and Leagros form the beginning of the development, which culminates in Sotades (p. 142).

The other drinking vessels, the kantharos, which is brandished by Duris' satyrs (Fig. 122), the skyphos, from which Euphronios' hetairai are drinking (Fig. 112) are only continuations and refinements of old shapes (Figs. 88, 43). The favourite drinking utensil is naturally the kylix, which even for the " little master " period in fabrication and exportation is at the head of the vases, and now not only receives its finest finish, but also through the abundance of specimens preserved and the richness of inscriptions renders the most valuable service to the historian.

On the Andokides amphora (Fig. 103), the psykters of Euphronios (Fig. 112), and Duris (Fig. 122), the shape with offset rim appears. This late specimen of the old type must have been more popular than the extant painted examples lead one to suppose, but was certainly far less usual than the shape with a single curve, which the red-figured style took over with the eye kylikes and in the most delicate way simplified and animated.

The history of these kylikes, like that of the big-bellied amphorae, begins with examples of mixed technique. Andokides actually extended his principle of the black-figured and red-figured halves of the vase to kylikes : but happily this procedure was extremely rare. In the early kylikes the mixture of technique is rather to be found in the fact, that in the interior the black-figured picture, which with its circle in the colour of the clay contrasted so decoratively with the black-covered edge, was still retained, while outside between the eyes, and gradually also in their place, figures were inserted in the colour of the ground. This procedure is *e.g.* connected with the names of the potters Nikosthenes, Pamphaios, Hischylos and Chelis, and with the painters' names Epiktetos and Psiax, and with the love-name Memnon. When Skythes paints the outside in black-figured technique and the inside in red-figured of a kylix (unsigned) dedicated to Epilykos, this is, like the procedure of Andokides, an exception, and a conscious divergence from the traditional relation. The transition to purely red-figured technique compels the artists to separate the interior from the black surroundings. Up to the Leagros period this separation is effected by a narrow ring in the ground of the clay, which they leave uncovered by black paint : on the kylikes the eye-decoration is gradually dropped. If one takes the signatures of the masters of this group together with those of the transitional kylikes and the contemporary big vases, the number of the painters' names comes to about a dozen, while the potters are far more numerous ; and thus in view of the mere accident of preservation and the anonymity of other palpable artistic personalities one can form an idea of the vigorous life, which then reigned in the Kerameikos, the quarter of Athens where the potters lived.

It is interesting to follow the process by which the early red-figured kylikes from very decorative beginnings rise to even greater freedom and objectivity. Even the insertion of the figure between the eyes, which comes from the Ionic 'Phineus' fabric, is meaningless and a mere decorative scheme ; and also, when he gives up the decoration with eyes, the painter likes to put one or three figures as central motive between the broad ornaments of the handles. Even the exterior pictures with numerous figures, which occur in the late period of the potter Pamphaios and in the full activity of the painter Oltos, are by no means free from decorative schematism; arrangement in a row and heraldry still play a part, and occasionally, as in the 'little master' style, winged horses or sirens take the centre of the representation. Even the old Ionic scheme of the horse-holding runner revives on a kylix of this group.

The interior too at first is still under strong decorative constraint.

Quite in contrast to the early Attic kylikes of the Klitias period and to the Spartan, which often take no regard to the space in the representation, the figure always adapts itself to the circular form, extends its masses to fit the space, often presses head and feet against the edge, and gives the interior a decorative and very animated appearance, to some extent comparable to a rotating wheel. One imagines the painters had studied and sketched the bending, crouching, running, twisting, and turning of handsome youths often only to get motives for their interior scenes. Skythes, the master of fine black-figured votive tablets on the Acropolis, who liked to dedicate his kylikes to his young colleague the painter Epilykos, in the interior of the kylix at Rome (Fig. 110) goes beyond this stage, and fills the space more loosely with the lyre held at right angles and the freely arranged knotted stick of his singing boy; and Epiktetos, who painted his wonderfully subtle figures in a long working life for various potters, Nikosthenes, Hischylos, Pamphaios, Python and Pistoxenos, in the late Python kylix in London (Fig. 111), under the influence of later masters, goes over to the two figure picture. One can see from their bodies that they are prior to the time of Euphronios and Euthymides. In his vigorous lyre-player, whom we may identify with his favourite Epilykos, Skythes does almost too much in the rendering of the chest-muscles and makes the abdominal muscles seen in front view, and rendered in thinned varnish, press against them in an impossible way ; Epiktetos, who is for a while disinclined for interior drawing, turns the breasts of his dancing women outwards, and in their space-filling movement reminds of old types. But the master of a Munich eye kylix has side-views of shields, and draws a kneeling leg in back view, so that the sole is visible and the calf almost disappears. Back views of the human body are given also in kylikes from the workshop of Kachrylion, which takes us over into the Leagros period just like the works of Phintias and Oltos, whom we already know. For Phintias soon outdoes the theft of the tripod of his early Deiniades kylix on a fine amphora at Corneto, and Oltos, the painter of the Pamphaios amphora and most of the Memnon kylikes, passes from the praise of Memnon to that of Leagros on the fine kylikes from Euxitheos' workshop.

The Leagros period might be described as the culminating point of the dramatic tension prevailing in the older red-figured style. In it Phintias breaks the archaic fetters of his youth, Euthymides creates his decisive works, and we see the development of the great master Euphronios, whom Euthymides boasts to have beaten on the Priam amphora (Fig. 105). All the three vases, which bear the signature of Euphronios as painter, praise the fair Leagros, *i.e.* the Munich Geryon kylix, which appeared in Kachrylion's workshop, which, like the Leagros kylikes of Oltos, has under the exterior scenes a band of circumscribed palmettes in the colour of the ground, the Petrograd psykter with the hetairai (Fig. 112) and the Paris calyx-krater with Herakles and Antaios (Fig. 113).

The harmonious indoors scene of the psykter in its quite

neat and sure drawing of the nude sets the finishing touch to the studies of Epiktetos (Fig. 111), Oltos (Fig. 104), and their contemporaries, and does the subject more justice than many pictures more advanced in perspective. The leg of the thirsty Palaisto disappearing in the background recurs in the Antaios scene, where the painter fully exhibits his anatomical knowledge, and shows as little regard for the concealing skin as other painters do for female drapery; the inner drawing is not even as usual put on in thinner colour. The composition of the scene is not very flexible. The struggle of the muscular but quite civilized Herakles with the rugged giant (whose right hand is a masterpiece of drawing) is the true theme, while the horrified women, who are almost old-fashioned in their drawing, serve like club, quiver and lion's skin, only as filling for the triangular wrestling scheme, which was probably borrowed. A band of palmettes, and another of palmette and lotus in the red-figured style, vigorously frame the bold picture. The reverse of the Antaios krater shows the artist well on the way to represent correctly the course of the abdominal muscles from the chest to the pudenda, and thus to give a convincing expression to the old distortion of the body. Unfortunately we cannot further follow Euphronios on this path in the light of signed vases, for the ten kylikes with his name, which fill the gap between the youth of Leagros and that of his son Glaukon, were only signed by him as potter and some of them were demonstrably handed over to others to paint. That a progressive artist like Euphronios in this whole period never again took brush in hand, is more than improbable, and among the unsigned vases of the succeeding period his more mature works must be represented.

The kylix made in the workshop of Sosias (Fig. 114) has been variously ascribed to Euphronios and to the painter

Peithinos : the remarkable work of art must rather belong to an unknown third person (the 'Sosias' painter). The composition filling the space suggests the old style, especially the pressing of the foot against the rim : but the boldly foreshortened right leg of Patroklos with the foot viewed from above, known also to Euthymides and to Phintias in his maturity, the full development of the bunches of drapery and the swallow-tail edges, and above all the extremely bold attempt to open the corner of the eye, lead us into the critical phase of the archaic red-figured painting, the Leagros period. Only an intense study of the model could lead this master so far from the beaten track ; that with the added names of Achilles and Patroklos he came into conflict with the Iliad, mattered little to him. Furthermore on the Sosias vase a technical innovation comes seriously into play, which is gradually adopted by Euphronios (Fig. 112), Euthymides (Fig. 107), Phintias and Hypsis (Fig. 106) ; the outline of the hair is no longer separated from the black ground by the old hard incised line, but by a narrow line of the colour of the ground. Within the kylikes, which praise the fair Leagros, a change takes place in the framing of the interior picture ; in place of the ring in the colour of the clay, of which occasionally they attempt to increase the effect by doubling, comes the maeander in different varieties, first simple and continuous (Frontispiece and Figs. 108, 115, 126), then ever more frequently in broken up shape (Fig. 116). The new frame comes e.g. on the London kylix, which by the hare-hunt gives such a natural motive for the space-filling movements of the running Leagros (Fig. 115). The Leagros of the kylix agrees so exactly with that of the Antaios krater, that one may ascribe this advance to Euphronios ; for the line of the ground giving the hair outline and the organic connection of chest and belly are beyond the stage of the krater in question.

125

A further step forward on the part of the same master may probably be seen in the Boston kylix, which praises both Leagros and Athenodotos (Fig. 108). Never perhaps was the inmost nature of the satyr so fully caught as in this fine example : he is squatting on the emptied pointed amphora and positively breathing out an aroma of wine and wantonness. His lifelike picture goes far beyond the Antaios krater, and a closely connected Athenodotos kylix in Athens actually carries this vivacity into the same subject, the wrestle of Herakles and Antaios.

If Euphronios thus surpassed himself one may believe him also responsible for the next step, the ' Panaitios ' stage, to which it is a very short distance from the Athenodotos kylikes. To the transition, that is about the end of the 6th century, belongs the Paris Theseus kylix, signed by Euphronios as potter but without love-name. The boldly drawn exterior seems to form the bridge to the style of the ' Panaitios ' master, that vigorous painter, perhaps identical with the later Euphronios, from whose hand comes the London Panaitios kylix with the signature of Euphronios as potter. The rich and ornamental interior (Frontispiece) is in a certain contrast with the exterior scenes, and is so closely connected with the early works of Duris, that we may enquire, whether Euphronios did not entrust the decoration of the interior to a talented pupil with a great tendency to elaboration. But perhaps this contrast is due only to the representative seriousness of the subject. Young Theseus, in order to receive his rightful position as son of Poseidon, has gone down to the bottom of the sea, and in the presence of Athena is greeted by Amphitrite.

The time of Panaitios and that of Chairestratos, which partly coincides with it, remove many hard features of the Leagros stage. The turnings of bodies lose all violence : in the frontal stand of both feet, and in the oblique view of the head, new possibilities are indicated. The pupil is now always in the inner corner of the eye, though the bold experiment of the 'Sosias' painter is not generally adopted. Above all a new current enters the drapery. The divisions of the chiton with patterns of folds gives way to a more natural and uniform distribution : the play of folds at the edges of the cloaks is generally emphasized by a thick pair of lines. These tendencies become complete in the later Chairestratos and the Hippodamas period, with which we get down to about 480 B.C.

The masters of this later date deal now quite freely and easily with the achievements of their predecessors : the old rude vigour gives way to ornamental elegance or swinging liveliness. The relation of figures to space also alters : the forms move more freely, are less confined by space, and are surrounded with air. Thus the free decoration of the Oltos amphora (Fig. 104) asserts itself once more. The small so-called 'Nolan' necked amphorae, and the popular amphorae of Panathenaic shape, only reserve one figure or group in the black surface. The fine and elegant effect of this 'Nolan' decoration often attacks other types of vases, to which is now added the bell-krater (cp. Fig. 123 centre).

Of these later masters, the one who keeps most the massiveness and dignity of the older style is the 'Kleophrades' painter, who grew up in the Leagros period and has furnished one of his works with the potter's signature of Kleophrades, son of Amasis. As an example of his style let us take the Munich pointed amphora belonging about to the Panaitios period : the passionate frenzy of frantic Maenads has never been more perfectly caught than in the back-tossed head of the rushing waver of the thyrsos (Fig. 117). The 'Kleophrades' painter was a pupil of Euthymides : but for a number of his contemporaries it can be shown that they won their spurs in the celebrated studio of

Euphronios. It is true that we only have evidence in an inscription of activity in the service of Euphronios for one painter denoted by name, and malicious accident has deprived us of all but the last four letters of his name. Onesimos, as his name is usually restored, combines in simple composition on his kylix riders and boys leading horses, and thus is the predecessor of the 'Horse' master. On the other hand the master of the Troilos kylix in Perugia, which Euphronios also signed as potter (the 'Perugia' master) inherited more of the fire and dramatic vigour of the 'Panaitios' master. His Munich Centaur kylix is worthy of the great teacher, and the interior (Fig. 126) is equally perfect as filling the space and as rendering animated life. The shield in profile view, which shows indication of shading, the Centaur's head, and especially the grandiose foreshortening of the horse-body, point beyond the Panaitios period.

To this group must have belonged the 'Brygos' painter, who in earlier works, e.g., in the clearly and vigorously composed Iliupersis in Paris (Figs 118 and 119), is still strongly inspired by the achievements of the Perugia master, and later develops the fiery vigour of his youthful period in ever more delicate and elegant shapes. He is fond of shaded shields, hairy bodies and cloaks adorned with spots. Perhaps the finest work of his maturity is the interior of the Würzburg kylix (Fig. 116), on which a young Athenian, supported by the hands of a girl, relieves himself of the wine he has imbibed too freely. The picture not only in its free adaptation to space and in the sure hand with which the movement of body and drapery is rendered, but especially in the fine animation of the expression, is a worthy last note of archaic art. The unsigned Vienna skyphos of the Brygos painter (Fig. 120) must be placed between the Paris and Würzburg kylikes. It also gives a fine picture full of life : Achilles has placed under the table the dead body of Hector, which he daily drags round the walls of Troy, is reclining at his meal, and talking to his charming cup-bearer, as if he did not hear the appeal of the old Priam for his son's corpse and did not see the presents brought in by the attendants. The clear dramatic disposition is as much in the manner of the master as the free pose of the cup-bearer with weight on one leg, and the delicate psychological animation of the countenances. The kylix in Corneto (Fig. 121), the outside of which has been interpreted as the secret departure of Theseus from the sleeping Ariadne, is at least closely related to the works of the ' Brygos ' painter. In the workshop of Euphronios the youthful Duris must also have been a pupil. For his earliest work, the Vienna kylix, with an arming scene, painted for the potter Python, is quite under the influence of the Panaitios master, and can only be recognized as the work of a painter of another tendency by the greater elegance and slimness of the figures, and the more schematic composition.

In the kylikes with the names of Panaitios and Chairestratos, it can still be traced to some extent, how out of the docile imitator of the Panaitios master comes the real Duris, the routine draughtsman, who puts down his elegant figures with almost academic objectivity and who cares more for the uniform decorative effect of his neat silhouettes than for complicated compositions of life. The pair of Berlin kylikes, perhaps made by Kleophrades, and the kantharos, on which Duris signs as potter and painter, show as plainly as possible this gradual realization of independence, and also pass more and more, though not finally, from the artificial fold packets of the chiton to a uniform system of wavy lines. How entirely Duris altered his style even during the Chairestratos period, is shown *e.g.* by the Vienna kylix, painted for Python with the contest for the Arms of

129

Achilles, which not merely in its more elegant shape, but also in drawing and the relation of the figures to the space, is widely distant from the arming scene on a kylix of the same workshop. The fine Eos kylix in the Louvre, which Duris painted for the potter Kalliades and dedicated to Hermogenes, the London Theseus kylix, and probably also the fine London psykter with the love-name Aristagoras (Fig. 122) belong to this period. The satyrs of this psykter, who instead of joining in procession play all kinds of unprofitable tricks behind the back of the leader of the chorus, need only be compared with their fellows on the Boston kylix, and one can recognize at once the routine hand and slighter artistic endowment of the master, but also the more elegant and easy draughtsmanship of the later time.

In the later period of the artist (about 480 B.C.) we must put along with their congeners the kylikes with the love-name Hippodamas, the finest of which is the Berlin school vase (Fig. 124). In the drapery of the teachers and pupils, who are here assembled in the class-room, nothing of archaic stiffness remains. If even the Leagros period had made the cloak folds come to a natural end, they now bend round their ends and pave the way for the " drapery eyes," which in the next period so naturally characterize the packings in the material.

The great development, which is evidenced for Duris by his many signatures, suggests considerations. We ask whether other masters too did not fundamentally change, and whether e.g. Euphronios did not develop out of the 'Leagros' stage to that of the 'Panaitios' master and the Perugia painter, and on his later works include the painter's signature in that of the potter's firm, i.e. whether works like the Munich Centauromachy (Fig. 126) do not represent a late phase of this gifted painter, who can be proved to have lived into the ' Glaukon ' period.

Of the other painters of this period, we must content ourselves with naming three, the Berlin master, Makron, and the Bronze-Foundry master. The ' master of the Berlin amphora ' even surpasses Duris in elegance, and is fond of introducing his slim elastic figures in ' Nolan ' style, *i.e.* isolated on a dark background.

Makron, who painted almost all the vases on which Hieron's signature as potter is found, studied by choice in the Palaestra, where boys performed gymnastics and were addressed by older men. A Berlin kylix (Fig. 123), like several works of his hand, introduces us to Bacchic revelry, an excited chorus of drunken and vigorously gesticulating maenads, whose bodies are not concealed by the rustling pomp of folds : the ' kolpos ' or fold of the chiton drawn up through the belt, which Brygos also is fond of, is more transparent than the upper and lower parts of the complicated garment. These figures in which all is life, movement and expression, should be compared with those of the Andokides painter or even those of Euphronios, in order to realize, how in these few decades the liberation from archaic stiffness and adherence to type was almost tempestuously accomplished.

We take leave of the archaic styles with the charming picture of an anonymous painter, the ' master of the bronze foundry,' who on a Berlin kylix (Fig. 125) transplants us into the interior of the workshop of a sculptor in bronze. A workman is poking the oven, another is handling the bellows, the assistant looks on, the master is working at a statue, not yet fully put together : so intimate is the contact with life in this scene. Everything interested the vase-painters of this time equally ; they have spread out before us human life, got their material from every quarter, and wherever they laid hold of it, it was interesting. How closely they came to grips with their subject, how they tried

131

to be clear, and to give a lively picture of what they saw, and how under their hands the object at once changed into the artistic type, the human body into the clearly defined study of the nude, the garment into a thing of decorative life, and an assemblage of human beings into an ornamental figure composition !

CHAPTER VI.

THE STYLE OF POLYGNOTOS AND PHEIDIAS

IN the studio of Euphronios the so-called 'Horse master' painted a kylix now in Berlin with the praise of the fair Glaukon. The outside is decorated in the usual red-figured technique with lively scenes of riders and stables, the inside (a youth and a girl) is rendered in outline, with coloured interior lines and surfaces, on the ground covered with a white slip. The progress in the rendering of bodies and drapery is unmistakeable; the oblique view of the female breast is almost correctly caught, the material of the cloaks is packed in lost folds with bent-round end. But even the whole conception of the figures goes far beyond the archaic art of the pre-Persian time: the proportions and faces have a touch of greatness, beside which all preceding art seems narrow and embarrassed. The simplification of the profile and the severe long lower part of the face essentially determine one's impression of the heads. A new period is announcing itself: a time of progressive naturalism and at the same time a period of noble greatness of style and exalted types. The statements of the ancients as to the great painting of this age, of Polygnotos and his company, lay stress on these qualities; not only the progress, which relieves the rendering of body and garment of the old stiffness, but the great Ethos of these paintings is praised. So with good reason we call the vase painting of the post-Persian generation Polygnotan, even if at the beginning of this epoch the influence of the great art is not felt so much as at its culmination.

133

GREEK VASE-PAINTING

The name of Glaukon, which we have met with on the Euphronios kylix of Berlin, recurs on a series of vases, almost always in the two-line arrangement, which comes now into vogue, and often in combination with his father Leagros' name. Lekythoi, or slender oil-flasks, which now become the regular offering for graves, and when so employed invariably use the white-ground technique of the Berlin kylix, afford several examples of this favourite's name, which has become the hinge of vase-chronology. On a Bonn fragment (Fig. 128), which in the older style has a domestic scene, not one taken from the cemetery, and paints the flesh in white, a woman is sitting in an arm-chair and putting on a golden necklace, which the handmaid in front of her has offered in a box. The face of this woman signifies a new world : the archaic types are discarded, the old traditions replaced by a quite individual almost portrait-like conception. The eye, which has hardly any traces of the old full-view and puts the pupil entirely into the open inner corner, gives the face a very natural and living effect, it is really looking : and the hair hanging out from the cap in confusion, the profile not dominated by any canon of beauty, and the drawing of the hands, show the painter penetrated by the same effort after truth. It is perhaps an idle question, what period inaugurates the history of Greek portraiture, since each innovation taken from the model individualizes the traditional type ; but it is just the vase-paintings of the post-Persian, Kimonian age, which went further than the later ones in thus individualizing. The woman of the Glaukon lekythos, the old woman on a skyphos in Schwerin from the workshop of Pistoxenos (Fig. 127) and on a loutrophoros in Athens, the head of a warrior from a krater in New York (Fig. 130) may be taken as symptoms of a very personal portraiture in the age of Kimon. The effort to get rid of the traditional ideal types led a series of these masters to recast even the divine figures with a strikingly individual, coarse and almost common effect. The master of the Boston 'Eos' kylix, a successor of Makron in Hieron's studio, makes his undistinguished goddess of the morning be carried off by a spindly street-lad ; the Demeter, who on a Munich hydria attends the departure of Triptolemos, betrays little of the sacred beauty of the motherly goddess ; and other vase-paintings have almost the effect of conscious caricatures of ideal types.

The new possibilities of 'Physiognomy' in differentiating character by the facial type, however, brought the expression of divine nature to its fullest expansion, and helped not merely to make men more human but also gods more divine. A London white-ground kylix from Rhodes (Fig. 129) is connected with the Bonn lekythos and the Berlin kylix of Euphronios by the common name of Glaukon. The goddess of love, riding through the air on her sacred bird, the goose, is of more than earthly beauty : her hands, not only the one with the flower but the unoccupied left hand, speak the same expressive language as her face and whole form. The effect of this picture is comparable to that of a song. Now for the first time the inner kinship of the art of words with that of pictures presses itself on the observer of works of art. No one will think of comparing the Geometric style with the Homeric Epic in value of expression, or the ornamental style of the 7th century with contemporary Lyric poetry, though one may see a reflection of Anacreontic and ballad feeling in the art of the later 6th century. But the weight of the Aeschylean pathos is as little to be mistaken in works of graphic and plastic art as the Sophoclean glow and pure beauty of line.

The more delicate animation, which this period could bestow on its forms, of itself pointed away from archaic loquacity and pleasure in narration. The genre scene is

135

certainly as old as the historical, and we have seen that there was no difference of principle. The nearer the red-figured style came, the more representations of feeling were combined with representations of action, and towards the end of the archaic style they are no longer rarities. With the new liberation of the style, especially with the enlivening of the eye, a different sort of inward feeling asserts itself. Figures devoid of action, occupied with themselves or contemplating another figure, are themes which the painters of lekythoi in particular were never tired of inventing; and in later times, when the cemetery scenes replaced the domestic ones on these vases, and the privacy of the indoor scenes was transferred to the visit to the grave, the harmony of soul between the visitor and the dead, whose living likeness fancy could not separate from the grave, often found an unspeakably intimate expression (p. 145).

The quantity of pictures of 'pure existence' does much to determine the altered aspect presented by post-Persian vase-painting. On the slim 'Nolan' amphorae and those with twisted handles, on the calyx-kraters and the bell-kraters often decorated on the mouth with a branch, on the 'stamnoi' and other vases, which are decorated like the 'Nolan,' the slender restful figures heighten the impression of quiet elegance. Thus the grandeur of the new style at the same time gets a marked decorative value, a value not without danger for the living rendering of reality. Greatness is not every man's affair, and the painters, who only took over externally the big forms and the lofty simplicity, and could not fill them with a life of their own, can only rank as decorative artists and should by the same right be called 'affected' as the refined masters of the Amasis period (p. 106). Even talented painters consciously gave up to decorative effect the reverses of their vases, which they adorn with quickly drawn motionless figures wrapped in cloaks.

THE STYLE OF POLYGNOTOS AND PHEIDIAS

The three Glaukon representations we have met with till now are pure pictures of ' existence.' The ' horse ' master dedicated to the same boy Glaukon a second kylix, the fragments of which, found on the Acropolis, represent the death of Orpheus at the hands of the Thracian women. The scheme, if one may speak of such, is in so far old, as the victor moving to the right attacks an opponent in kneeling position also moving to the right and looking round ; but an infinite nobility is poured over the old type, and the fight is carried through with dramatic weight, though in the faces of the fighters the inward excitement is not reflected, as on later works of the same hand. Yet, as on the Aphrodite kylix (Fig. 129) the living expression of the eye is already strengthened by the line of the upper lid.

In place of the very fragmentary Orpheus kylix, the fight in a contemporary picture may show the progress, which scenes of dramatic movement attain in Polygnotan times. The slaying of Aktaion by the divine huntress Artemis was brought to great effect by the Pan master, so called from the reverse of the same Boston bell-krater (Fig. 131). In the stiff folds of the cloak of Artemis this vigorous and original painter betrays his descent from the archaic style, which can be plainly followed in his works, always full as they are of dramatic life. Otherwise there is little archaic in this picture. The long lower part of the face, which lends the heads their severity, the folds running themselves out, which assert themselves even in the chiton, the surely drawn fore-shortened foot of Artemis, the lower legs of Aktaion disappearing in the background, show the progressive master ; the suggestive effect of the composition, and the urgent language of the gestures are quite in the spirit of the noble new style.

With the Centaur psykter in Rome (Fig. 132) we get

137

perhaps beyond the bloom of Glaukon's beauty, and what reminds us of old times in the grotesque movement of the battle scene is probably only individual failings of the master, which he outweighs by many innovations. The three-quarters view of the face, the fore-shortening of the shield, the motive of the falling man seen from behind, are significant of the struggle with perspective; the bestial lust for battle speaks out of the eyes of the attackers as does the penetrating pain of the wounded; and the pathos of the gestures is at least post-archaic. The impression of this vase is remarkably determined by the experiments in colouring, which the master undertakes with help of thinned colour : the helmets, greaves, and hides he has made dark in contrast with the human skin, he has given an effect of light to the material of the hair of head and beard, and rounded the horses' bodies by shading.

These novelties of the somewhat crude and quaint master are only intelligible as reflection of a great painting, which struggled with problems of expression and light, as is expressly testified for the art of the great Polygnotos and his contemporaries. Naturally at no time were vase-painters entirely uninfluenced by the achievements of the great art. But just now in the sixties of the 5th century, this borrowing made itself felt more than ever, and enticed the vase-painters often beyond the limits of their branch of art. This comes not only from the overpowering impression of the great personalities among the painters of this period, but especially from the fact, that wall-painting now struck out new bold paths, on which vase-painting could follow it less than ever.

Among the vase-pictures, which very strongly echo these new strains, are the later works of the 'horse' master. The interior of the Penthesileia kylix (Fig. 134) only enclosed by a delicate branch, the master did not paint as in

138

the kylikes of Berlin and Athens on white ground, but he heightens the red-figured technique by the application of thinned black glaze, by dull red and light grey surfaces, with brown and white additions, and by applications of gold. The four figures which are forced into this circle almost burst the frame, not merely by the disproportion of their tall forms, but still more by their inner greatness and passion. In the midst of the battle-field, where the sword rages, and the ground lies full of corpses, Achilles has overtaken the Amazon queen, and furious with rage, plunges his sword in her heart : however much her hands and eyes plead for mercy, it is too late.

The features of Penthesileia betray more of inner life than those of Orpheus : and on a second Munich kylix, on which Apollo in presence of Ge slays her son Tityos, the master has gone a step further in physiognomy. The three faces are as convincingly graduated in expression as for example those on the beautiful 'Lament for the dead,' by a contemporary master, in Athens.

On the big interior of his kylikes (Fig. 134) the 'horse' master could give freer play to his genius than on the exteriors, which, as in the kylikes of Berlin and Athens, he adorned with pretty scenes from the stable. The contrast between the great round pictures with their fine technique, and the lightly sketched exteriors, is so great, that some have thought of two artists working in the same studio, who divided the work, so that the 'horse' master would be different from the Penthesileia master ; but the white-ground exterior of the Orpheus kylix seems to build the bridge. It is certainly characteristic that the exteriors of kylikes in this period no longer tempted talented painters to such lively compositions, as in the days of the Brygos and Perugia painters, and that even in the lifetime of the great Euphronios the paratactic decorative

139

style most consistently prepared by Duris laid hold of these exteriors. The new style required big surfaces, and the most faithful reflexions of wall-painting are to be found on large vases.

The most famous of these great Polygnotan vases is the Paris calyx-krater from Orvieto (Fig. 135), the figures of which, apart from Athena and Herakles, have not yet been certainly identified. From the expectant attitude of the figures it has been suggested that the picture represents the start of the Argonauts, or the preparation of the Attic heroes for the battle of Marathon. The great mythological scene is at any rate in the manner of the new period, which no longer has the preference of the ancients for the crisis of action but rather depicts preparation and after-effect, reflection on the deed accomplished and rest from action. That a Polygnotan wall-painting preceded the vase-painting in this psychologically refined conception, may be regarded as proved. For the figures not only appear in all sorts of bold foreshortenings, front and side views, not only surprise us by an abundance of motives, which are quite beyond previous vase-painting, but also show a series of peculiarities, which are expressly described as innovations of the great fresco-painter. When the figures of the krater open their mouths and show their teeth, when the stationary interior folds, the so-called drapery eyes have shadows painted in them, this can only be explained as imitation of the great painters, and similarly the gnashing of teeth and the shading of the horses' bellies on the Centaur psykter. The Argonautic krater shows this dependence very strongly in its composition. Great painting had not only graduated the parts of the body in deep spatial layers, but transferred this novel deepening to the arrangement of its groups, distributing the actors over hilly country, which either elevated the figures of the background or often partly concealed them. It is clear that an art, which characterized the rounding of shields and bodies and the recesses of drapery by the distribution of light and shade, also gave actuality and effect of depth to the landscape by shading, though in primitive fashion, and a series of ' Polygnotan ' vases proves the fact, by making flowers, bushes and plants spring out of the ground. It is true the painter of the Argonaut krater does not go so far, but he shows more strikingly than any other vase-painter the landscape of Polygnotan paintings, which, not forgetting the surface effect of vase-decoration, he does not shade but only indicates in outline by the incising tool. That in other ways, too, he altered his pattern to suit the technique of vase-painting, is proved by the freedom in the use of colour and perspective, which on other specimens of this period burst the barriers of vase-painting.

Both encouraged and warned by such examples, one must look through the vase-painting of this period for other traces of Polygnotan painting, especially on vases which agree in subject with the wall-paintings of which we have accounts, and not only in the freedom named, but also in the inferiority of the execution to the conception, show of what spirit they are the offspring. One can never expect copies. The very fact that exact replicas never occur among the Polygnotan types, shows that the vase-painters dealt with the borrowed property according to their own individuality and for their definite purpose. So the two cases we have selected must be judged individually. The ' Penthesileia ' master was probably stimulated to his treatment of the theme by a big Amazon painting ; but the clever painter not merely translated this impulse into his own brilliant technique and adapted it to his circular field, but also extended over it his personal great feeling, and

141

translated the picture into his personal style, so that it has the effect of a natural continuation of his earlier works. The ' Argonaut ' master had no concern with this great ' Ethos' or the delicate polychrome technique. He borrowed more superficially, took an extract from the big scene of his model in his strong relief-lines, and emphasized the individual characteristics rather than the dash of the original. In realism, his bearded hero holding a spear is not inferior to the contemporary warrior of the New York krater (Fig. 130). Great painting went on tempestuously developing, and in the next age burst its fetters of colour and space in a manner which could not but deter even the boldest vase-painter from imitation, if he were not to shake off every sane regard for the preservation of his surface-effect. So reflexions of wall-painting on vases become rarer, and the ' Polygnotan ' vases remain an episode.

Naturally there were many vase-painters who did not enter this dangerous ground : nay, the majority did not do so. With many the avoidance of a big surface went so far that they divided the outside of a calyx-krater or big ' aryballos ' into two friezes and filled them with small figures in defiance of constructive considerations. Out of the series of these ' little masters,' who beside the big-figure painters continued the traditions of the elegant style, let us mention e.g. the painter who decorated the box signed by the potter Megakles (Figs. 136-7) with charming scenes from women's apartments, and the lid with five comic hares ; or the author of the girl plying the top on a white-ground kylix of the potter Hegesibulos (Fig. 133), a potter who was active as early as the'Leagros period ; and especially Sotades, from whose workshop came not only plastic vases in the shapes of horses, sphinxes, knuckle-bones, crocodiles devouring negroes, etc., but also white-ground kylikes of most elegant shape, whose exquisite interiors, like the friezes of those

142

drinking vessels, lead us to the beginning of the age of Pheidias.

This transition is also accompanied by some painters' signatures, which become rarer, the more the individual performances of vase-painters are cast in the shade by the great art. The signatures do not present us with the first artists of the time. Hermonax is somewhat smooth and tedious, and Polygnotos, the namesake of the great painter, to judge from the mixed nature of his unoriginal style, must have lived by borrowing. His pelike from Gela is a Polygnotan vase with an Amazon scene ; on the London stamnos, to be dated about the middle of the century, advanced and old-fashioned types are combined in an unpleasing fashion.

Anonymous masters better represent the transition from Polygnotos to Pheidias. The master of a krater with a dancing scene in Rome (the 'Villa Giulia' master), is not distinguished for temperament and progressiveness, but is rather a correct and academic individual ; but the neatly drawn scenes of his krater and stamnoi, in the noble bearing of the figures and the manner in which they gaze at each other, betray the approach of a new ideal of man. Much more talented is the master, who on a pointed amphora at Paris combined the wonderful group of two Maenads (Fig. 138) with a scene of Bacchic revelry, as Amasis did almost a century before (Fig. 98). The two girls are of truly royal dignity, like each other in this, but subtly distinguished in expression. The three-quarter view of the head is almost devoid of harshness, and only the ladle-shaped under lip connects her with the Polygnotan female heads.

How even the drapery becomes a vehicle of expression and every fold breathes the greatness of the whole picture, may become clearer if we look at the 'Eriphyle' of a pelike at Lecce (Fig. 139), with which we also pass the middle of the century. This picture must be compared to the

143

Corinthian Amphiaraos krater (Fig. 66) to see, how in the interval of 120-130 years the soul of art has changed. The later master represents not the dramatic culmination of the story but the psychological climax, when Polyneikes offers to the wife of Amphiaraos the seductive necklace, for which she will send her husband to death. As often on vases of this period, two figures stand calmly facing one another, but they are here united by most delicate psychology ; Eriphyle, simply attired in plain peplos, is full of an inner life which circulates through her body to the finger-tips. This harmonious union of a monumental type with intimate feeling is at the beginning of the most Greek period of Greek art-history , the most human period of the history of mankind, the age of Pheidias.

If we name the following decades of the history of vase-painting after Pheidias, we do not mean that he was in very close relations with the art of the vase-painters. But the artist, who in the Parthenon frieze introduced that inconceivable nobility of form, who in the West side of the frieze developed the play of lines to new greatness, to heighten it in the pediment to a great outburst of passion, impressed this age so much with his nature that one cannot imagine the vase-paintings as unaffected by this powerful influence.

Never was Greek art so much an art of expression as at this period. As if in response to the search for a word to describe this new expression, the beautiful musical pictures of the time present themselves. Since the Geometric style art had continually represented musical performers, but it was reserved for the age of Pheidias to give pictorial expression to the effect of musical sounds on men. The krater from Gela (Fig. 140) belongs to the early Periclean age ; the sure touch in the rendering of a twist of the body and its rounded form is now a matter of course even in the hasty execution of a second-rate draughtsman ; the head type gets the

144

square outline, the shortened jaw, the long drawn nose, which are characteristic of the age of Pheidias ; the repetition of the epithet *kalos* shows that the custom of inscribing a love-name is dying out. About contemporary is the London amphora with twisted handles (Fig. 141) with the Muses Melusa and Terpsichore and the bard Musaios. Orpheus among the Thracians and Terpsichore in a reverie with the harp are purely pictures of lyric feeling.

As if music had tamed them, the vase-pictures of the Periclean age change their nature. All crudities have gone : the too bold foreshortenings and the realistic details taken from great paintings are less obvious : nothing any longer disturbs the free play of the lines. The conception of men rises to its highest possible point. The figures on the Munich stamnos (Fig. 146) are not merely masterpieces of fully developed drawing but also ideal types of pure free humanity. Movements are often merely motives of beauty : the fold style combines a new naturalism with the most monumental effect.

This new spirit also animates the finest of the white-ground lekythoi, whose proper history begins in the Glaukon period (p. 134) and cannot be traced far beyond the 5th century. In their first period they had preferred to render domestic scenes, representations from the female apartments. But the purpose of these grave vases continually asserts itself more and more. The ferryman of the dead appears, to take goodly men into his bark ; the brothers Sleep and Death dispose of the corpse (Fig. 142) ; Hermes, the conductor of souls, waits to be followed ; the dead man laments for his life. But the domestic scenes have given place to the walk to the grave ; and the visit to the tombstone, beside which the dead man stands or sits as if alive, becomes the typical subject of the lekythoi. The special technique of these vases produces an effect often very

145

different from the red-figured style, especially since the white filling of the outlines (p. 134) is dropped. The employment of glaze-colour in the rendering of outlines, and the transition to brush-painting, with which from the first surfaces had been covered in different varieties of colour, lead afterwards to an unusual individualization of the line. One cannot say that this technique approximates the lekythoi to the effect of wall-painting as much as it severs it from red-figured vase-painting. Only a few exceptional late specimens in their pictures operating freely with light and shade burst the bounds of vase-decoration, and show clearly with what good sense the vase-painters renounced competition with the great art, which now victoriously solves the problems of full perspective, of giving the effect of depth in space, with the gradation of dimensions, and the contrasts of light and dark.

In a Boston lekythos (Figs. 143 and 144) we have an 'existence' picture in the manner of the new period (p. 136). The dead warrior stands in Polygnotan attitude, with bent arm resting on his hip (cp Fig. 135, last to left), beside his altar-shaped tomb, and looks over it to the girl, who without perceiving him approaches with funeral offerings. One notices in the treatment of the nude, that he is the product of an age which already had the perspective sense : so vividly do the few lines of his contour, his muscles, and his knee-pan, give the suggestion of a rounded body ; and also the drawing of the female nude, which accident has freed from the drapery added in perishable dull paint, in its very realistic outline goes beyond anything previous. Since the Circe and Phineus kylikes, and the numerous black-figured and red-figured pictures of bathing, dancing, and drinking hetairai, art had busied itself with the naked bodies of women as much as of men : and where nudity could not be represented, it indicated the outlines of the body through

146

the cover of the drapery (p. 119). For Polygnotos we have the express tradition of women with transparent garments, and on the Argonaut krater even Athena's grand forms are indicated; the great liberator of wall-painting must also have been a pioneer in the drawing of the female body. The new style here too brings perfection and fills the form of women with its noble greatness and simplicity. That it too, in contrast with the 4th century, eschews all that is typically feminine, soft and unformed, is a proof how strong was the ideal of male beauty.

A London lekythos (Fig. 142) also represents a dead soldier at the grave. The winged brothers Sleep and Death with tender hand dispose of his corpse, as they do with the dead Sarpedon in the Iliad : and the lekythos-painter took his type also from the Sarpedon pictures; the young warrior who had fallen far from his country, should on the vase have the same boon of burial in his native soil, as was granted by Zeus to the Lycian king. The fine type was then divested of its proper meaning and received a more general signification. The London vase, which uses lustreless colours for the outlines of its figures also, must be somewhat later than the Boston vase, although the new technique, that is pure brush technique, went on for a time beside the old. Though stylistic estimates now become difficult, one fancies in the wonderful vigour of the drawing, and in the stronger individuality of the hair, that one is nearer to the period of the Parthenon pediments than in the somewhat more austere Boston group. Where the way led may be shown by the woman sitting on the steps of a tomb on a lekythos in Athens (Fig. 145), which not only by the strongly plastic suggestion of the outline goes beyond the Pheidian period proper, but also in the grandiose heightening of the simple motive shows itself as one of the works which take up and cast in new moulds the pathos of

147

the Parthenon pediments. Every line in the very individual drawing of the woman, who is supporting her left hand and lifting her garment with her right, while her feet are unruly in submitting to the sitting posture, is animated by passionate unrest.

Though the age of Pheidias liked pictures of feeling with quiet figures like the music-scenes, the Munich stamnos and the lekythoi, it did not exhaust itself in them. Beside the vases with large figures, there are others, which continue to cultivate the elegant style and prepare the way for a class which flourishes in the last decades of the century. Little jugs with nursery scenes, pomade boxes with pictures of female life, globular unguent pots with lekythos-like mouth are the principal vehicles of this style, and the " Eretria " master is a typical representative. On great and small vases we find scenes of animated motion, passionate scenes of conflict, which on their side too, share in the nobility of the style of the age. The brutal vigour and hardness of old motives seems broken, softened, often almost takes a turn to elegance. The order of the large compositions with its arrangement of the figures over one another and indication of the broken ground by lines closely follows the Polygnotan system. But while the Polygnotan depth in space was produced by a naturalistic tendency, which soon led to complete freedom in the great art, it is continued by the vase-painters as a mere principle of distribution and space-filling, i.e., it receives a decorative character.

One of the finest pictures of movement from this period decorates a stamnos at Naples (Fig. 147) : women who are sacrificing before a tree-trunk dressed out as Dionysos and dancing to the tambourine. The exact dating of this picture, like the whole chronology of the late and post-Pheidian vases, is a matter of dispute : but this much is certain, that it cannot be understood except as a near echo of the art of

148

the Parthenon pediments. Into the noble line-drawing of the middle style of Pheidias has come a new passionate movement, which draws the contour in more violent curves, dissolves the hair in strong waves, throws the drapery into great folds, and enlivens the clinging parts with restlessly curving inner folds. The upper garment of Dionysos is given rich effect by long border zig-zags, interspersed stars and an embroidered wreath, the expression of his eyes is strengthened by emphasis on the upper lid. Details added in white and liberal use of thinned black heighten the coloured effect. This new style with its marked enhancement of the lines is the later style of Pheidias, a reflection of the last and highest development of the Parthenon master, which pointed Attic art into new paths, and lived its life out and died in the school of Pheidias.

The amphora with twisted handles at Arezzo (Fig. 148) must be in close connection with the last phase of the Pheidian style and cannot be far removed from the Naples stamnos. Its shape enriches the type of the Terpischore vase in London (Fig. 141) by sharper profiling of the mouth and foot, but does not yet draw the lower part into the dull curve, which robs the amphorae and bell-kraters of the end of the century of strong and taut effect. Similarly the scene, the wild career of Pelops and Hippodameia over the sea, heightens the tendencies of Pheidian art without succumbing to the palsy which can be felt in the style of Meidias. The divine horses, the gift of Poseidon, emit sparks of the fire of the steeds on the pediments; the majestically animated attitude of Hippodameia reminds one of the Athenian lekythos (Fig. 145); in Pelops every line is full of passion and bold movement. Here too the draperies are rich and elaborate, the restless billowing of the folds is more marked than on the Naples stamnos, and the flowing chiton folds, which cling close to the body, pre-

149

L

pare for the exaggeration dear to post-Pheidian sculpture and painting. Not only does the drawing of individual forms show a plastic conception of space, but the whole scene is inconceivable without a contemporary big painting with considerable landscape capacities : from the tree-clad hilly coast the chariot rushes out upon the deep sea.

In fiery impetus only one of the vase-paintings of this period can compare with the Pelops vase, the somewhat later Naples fragment of a Gigantomachia (Figs. 149-151). An invention of truly Titanic force, which is also echoed on other later vases, must be the basis of this picture, and even the unusual division (unsuited to vases) by an arch points to a model from another branch of art. In a rocky landscape the fight for existence of the gods and the sons of the earth-goddess takes place in the early morning, when Helios is rising on the vault of heaven and Selene is sinking down into ocean, as on the east pediment of the Parthenon. The bold movements, the twistings and bendings of the combatants, the 'lost' profile, the swellings and packings of the skin and muscles are rendered with sure touch. The plastic effect of the middle line of chest and abdomen is increased by doubling, and horizontal folds bring out the lower part of the forehead, the locks of hair and tips of hide flutter as if they were alive; the breasts of the earth-goddess are modelled out of the drapery as if bare, the eyes are deep-set, the underlips project.

That the rendering of the female body was now not less accomplished than that of the male, beside the lekythos in Athens, a picture of a different order may show. On an Oxford jug appears in the spaciousness favoured by these vases an old theme, Satyr and Nymph (Fig. 154). One can scarcely realize the nobility of Pheidian conception more fully than by comparing this scene with the Phineus kylix (Fig. 74) and its congeners. What early ages had repre-

150

sented with drastic humour, is here refined and given a
soul : even the Satyrs and Centaurs, the rugged monsters of
the woods and mountains, are tamed by the new spirit which
will not any longer endure brutality and obscenity.

The sleeping nymph Tragodia is not only correctly
observed in her foreshortening, in movement and distribution of the weight of the body, she is also the vehicle of a
wonderful feeling. The picture, which immediately pre-
pares for the works of the Meidias painter and the
' Pronomos ' master, and beside the great style of the
Pelops and Giant vases shows us the continuance of the
refined and elegant style, cannot have been produced long
after Pheidias' death.

The time of the School of Pheidias, of whose best works
we have been introduced to a selection, gives us again a few
artists' names. The painter Aison gives us a Madrid kylix
with the exploits of Theseus, which must be about contemporary with the Giant vase. On the Theseus of the interior
the hair is dissolved into lively curls, which stand out dark
on a lighter ground, and the plastic swelling of the belly goes
to the utmost limit of what is possible ; in his protectress
Athena we see already the contrast between the leg that
bears the weight and is covered by hanging folds, and the
free leg, which is closely covered by the drapery ; which is
exaggerated by Aristophanes, whom the potter Erginos
employed, just as is the hair with light under-painting, and
the chiton clinging as if moist and blowing back. Aison,
who began his activity even in Pheidian days, draws more
elegantly than his younger colleague, but neither master
initiated a new development of kylix painting. The greatness of both lay in exploiting as artizans accessible types.

With the works of Aristophanes we probably go further
from the time of Pheidias than with the Naples fragment :
the works of the ' Meidias ' painter take us to the time of

the Nike balustrade, *i.e.*, the two last decades of the 5th century. They too are an echo of the art of the Parthenon pediments, but in travelling along the road this echo has lost its vogour. On the unsigned Adonis hydria in Florence (Fig. 152) all the figures exuberate in lazy grace and fine motives of beauty. Particularly the groups, Adonis in the lap of Aphrodite, and Hygieia with Paidia, remind us of the Parthenon, the wonderful melting forms of the 'Fates' and other pediment figures. But what there was born of passion, is here become fashion, and is playfully treated. The excitement of the faces with wide nostrils, the bowing and bending of bodies conscious of their beauty, the supporting of arms and play of fingers, the whole extent of the carelessly united society on the wavy hill-lines (p. 141) in spite of all its grace has something of the formula about it. The style of the drapery is certainly an indication of the weakening of earlier vigour. The many and over elegant broken-up folds, which cling unnaturally close to breast and free leg, the curling of the cloak folds, and the independent movement of the tips, is a long way off the Parthenon pediments, which inaugurate this enhancement of style, but without loss of vigour and by a kind of natural evolution. The effort for fine effect, which is expressed in the rich patterning, is in noticeable contrast to the restlessness of the drapery. A certain inclination to pomp is characteristic of the post-Pheidian stvle. The raised gilt details of the clay, which we know already on the white ground lekythoi (Fig. 134), the box of Megakles (Fig. 137) and the works of the Eretria master (p. 148), are now in high honour, and are plentifully employed on the Adonis vase.

The Meidias painter also produced a series of similar pure pictures of ' existence ' on hydriae, *e.g.*, the fair Phaon, the singer ' Thamyris,' Paris with the goddesses, the Eleusinian deities, and decorated other vases also in this manner. These scenes, on which the figures move less vigorously than the lines, are more successfully rendered than the pathos of the scene of abduction on the London hydria signed by the potter Meidias. He was no bold progressive artist; his technically exquisite and very delicately drawn pictures recast in new shapes the new phenomena of art: in him the series of masters of the type of the 'Sotades' painter and the Eretria master comes to an end.

His contemporary, who may after the chief figure of the Satyric play vase at Naples be called the 'Pronomos' master, likes figures of 'existence' in pretty poses, but he draws them with more spirit and does more justice to the vehement style of his time. On the Naples vase, a showy volute-krater with rich profiling, he puts on the obverse the cast of an Attic theatrical performance in two almost equal rows one above the other, and thus starts a principle of composition which was taken up by the vase-painting of Lower Italy (Fig. 158). Liberal use is made of thinned colour, the centre of the scene is denoted by a white figure, the luxuriantly ornamented dresses confuse the general impression. In respect of shape and decoration one may speak of a decay of the finer tectonic sense, which reminds us surprisingly of the vases of Lower Italy. The perspective side-view of the footstool and of the tripod column are liberties taken by the great art, which generally Attic vase-painters consciously avoid so as to keep to the surface treatment.

The tripod-column, which transplants us into the Theatre of Athens, as the Athena of the Panathenaic vases to the Acropolis, recurs after Polygnotan times often in the midst of mythological scenes, and brings the vases, which show it, anyhow in relation to dramatic exhibitions.

It has been proposed to recognise the effect of the stage

on vase-painting, *e.g.* in the increased pomp of the dresses. This effect might at the most have taken place indirectly ; for that the vase-painters often took as their patterns votive paintings of victorious Choregi, is more than probable. And in general one may draw conclusions as to the great art from many a fine invention, which is seen on vase-paintings at second-hand, *e.g.* from the Bacchic scenes on the reverse of the ' Pronomos ' vase. This conclusion is certainly also justified in view of the Talos vase (Fig. 153) which transforms the mighty echoes of the late Pheidian art into the pompous, as the Meidias vases into the ornamental-elegant. The vase-shape is closely allied to that of the ' Pronomos ' : the central figure in white, so popular in this period, recurs, and in its spatial effect is enhanced by shaded modelling far above the proportions of the other figures, which show plainly the conscious restraint of the vase-painters. Though the ' Talos' master altered the composition of his pattern to suit his vase, he must have preserved with tolerable faithfulness the grandiose invention of the centre group ; the passionate impetus, which fills the whole scene and catches even the cloaked figures of the reverse, is here most convincing.

With this fine masterpiece, which almost exaggerates the element of show, not separated by more than two decades from the Parthenon pediment, we close the history of the vases that show the style of Pheidias. Nay, one may regard the proper history of Greek vase-painting as closed with these post-Pheidian vases. Not merely does the potter make his vases untectonic by excessive profiling and elaborate extension, but the painter too, interrupts the unity of the vase-surface with the white-painted and plastically modelled central figure ; thus in a sense the silhouette style is declared bankrupt.

CHAPTER VII.

LATE OFFSHOOTS

W E should unnaturally shift the centre of gravity in our narrative if we treated the late period of Greek vase-painting with anything like the same fulness as its development from the Geometric to Meidias. The fully developed and often almost playfully treated vase-shapes give no longer any really tectonic ground for the silhouette style, which had exhausted the qualities compatible with its inward nature : the elegance of the vases feels the pictorial decoration to be a burden, as does the style of the figures feel the tectonic compulsion. Even in the last third of the 5th century examples are multiplied of the transition to free brush technique. The Pelops amphora (Fig. 148) adorns its black neck with a sphinx added in white, the Talos vase (Fig. 153) and with it a multitude of other vases seek to fix the impression by a white central figure, to which the others rendered in ordinary technique are only a pale foil. In the course of the 4th century this foil too, was dropped, and black glazed vases of elegant shape were decorated only with figures or ornaments loosely added in white. The brush technique, both the black of Boeotian vases (p. 110) and the white of Attic and Lower Italian, made a new development in ornamentation, which culminates in spiral tendrils and branches with depth of space, in combination of figures and foliage of plastic effect. Besides these freely decorated vases the red-figured long continue. But the centre of gravity of the manufacture lies no longer in Athens. Even in the time of Pheidias the Attic school sent a branch to Lower Italy, which took root in the Periclean

155

colonies of Lucania, extended to various places in Lucania, Campania, Apulia, and Southern Etruria, and soon grew up as a strong plant. In this production, which in the 4th century completely supplanted Attic importation, few really original artists took part, who all seem to belong to the early period, and perhaps were emigrated Athenians; the master of the Paris 'Tiresias' krater is one of them. From the early group, in which good Attic tradition is strongly felt, we select two bell-kraters. The full, and rather empty heads, the very general conception of the divine types leave us no doubt as to the Italian origin of the Paris ' Orestes ' vase found in Lucania (Fig. 156), while the wonderful group of the sleeping Erinyes, Klytemnestra urging them to vengeance, and the purified Orestes, show us not only a fine model but a clever hand. From the drawing and shape of the vase it may very well belong to the end of the 5th century, like the closely analogous London krater (Fig. 157). This vase with much humour introduces to us one of the favourite Italian farces (the Phlyakes) and begins a long series of similar representations from different workshops. Thus *e.g.* the painter Assteas painted two Phlyax vases, one of which in comic parody gives the violation by Aias of Kassandra, while the other is a serious theatrical scene, which with its detailed rendering of the stage clearly demonstrates the influence of the drama on vase-painting.

The activity of this painter, who from the stiff variety of the style and the localities of the finds must be localized in South Campania, belongs to a later phase, which does not concern us. For the more these Italo-Greek vases in shape, decoration and representation develop local peculiarities and depart from their purely Attic starting point, the less do they belong to our survey, which excludes provincial varieties. Out of the mass of Lower Italian vases of the 4th century, which in shape partly run parallel with the Attic, partly develop noticeably baroque and locally limited peculiarities, which in their chiefly sepulchral representations, influenced by Orphic-Dionysiac cults, often fall into coarseness, stiffness, or effeminate insipidity, let us take only one example. The Boston volute krater, $1\frac{1}{4}$ metres high (Fig. 158) belongs to a group of Apulian grand vases, which elongate the shape of the Talos vase (Fig. 153) and add rich ornament in white colour. On the reverse bearers of offerings above one another in the favourite borrowed motives (sitting, standing, running, leaning on a pillar, drawing up one foot) surround a white-painted Heröon with the dead man : the obverse combines a similar building with a mythological scene, the slaying of Thersites by Achilles, and thus gives a mythical prototype to the dead man, for whose grave the vase is designed. The liberal use of white paint, the 'black ground' ornamentation of the neck and foot with branches and tendrils are progressive elements, which lead the way for Hellenistic products like the Apulian Gnathia vases ; in the increased pathos of the faces is traced, though provincially coarsened, the stronger weight given to sentiment in the 4th century ; and the perspective rendering of the building operating with light and shade, which often extends to the ornament, points to a period, which had won complete freedom in space, and certainly could distribute figures over the landscape more naturally than the vase-painter, who filled the tall space with them only in a superficially decorative way.

Sentiment and light, the great achievements of 4th century art, were the ruin of the decorative silhouette style, whose figure world can admit of pathos, as little as the bursting of its vase sides by perspective views corresponds to its surface decoration. Even in Athens, where out of the successors of the Meidias, Pronomos and Talos styles an after-bloom developed (Figs. 155 and 159), which from the

157

rich exports in the Black Sea is usually called the Kerch style, the new tendencies of art were fatal to the red-figured style. To be sure this was in a different direction to Lower Italy. The figure world of the elegant Attic vases, which in the new naturalness of motives and drapery, in the strong emphasis on female forms, is far removed from the types of Pheidias, betrays little of the enhanced pathos of the great painting, which one would have to deduce from the sculpture of Skopas and Praxiteles, even if it were not expressly witnessed to by literary tradition. From the same finer decorative sense the Attic masters made no use of the full perspective of their time, and interrupted the vase-surface neither by buildings or ornaments drawn in perspective nor by composition in several planes, but following the old manner simply arranged above and beside each other on the surface their generally large and restful figures. As in the post-Pheidian style they like to pick out single figures by white colour, and do not despise gilded additions, nay, they even often heighten the decorative effect of colour by the application of light blue, green and rose, occasionally also by figures in relief and painted (as Xenophantos did in his aryballos with hunting Persians, meant for Eastern customers, in signing which he emphasizes his Athenian citizenship). The varying shades of the colour scale give one an inkling of the new problems of light, which were certainly struggling for expression not only in sculpture ; in the drawing of the figures, rendered in strong relief strokes, nothing of this is observed. Thus the ' Kerch ' masters ensure to their vases a finer general aspect than the Southern Italians, just as their commonest figures are distinguished from the Italian by a certain nobility ; but they are far behind the huge advances of the great art, which now in its methods of expression attained the heights perhaps of Titian and Tintoretto, and have an *arrieré* effect, listless and dull. Just as the new style could express itself better by the applied than by the reserved ornamentation, which in spite of new formations has a stiff and lifeless effect, so too the red-figured style, which as is proved by finds at Alexandria, continued to exist down into the early Hellenistic age, was no longer the congenial vehicle of the expression of its age ; and it was only seldom that notable personalities attempted to practise it.

Rightly recognising that the days of the draughtsman and his decorative figure style were past and gone, the ceramic workshops of the late 4th century, and the Hellenistic, which appeared in several spots of the now decentralized Greek world, more and more gave up the red-figured technique. The great increase of the means of colouring, which is to be assumed for the late painting, the complete suppression of formal tendencies in favour of impressionism did not permit the silhouette style even a subsidiary place. The future belonged to free brush technique, that which painted in black, and that which had a black ground (pp. 110 and 157).

The figured world, the representations, no longer play any part ; the Hellenistic painters prefer to put on their elegant, often playfully treated vases tendrils, festoons, hanging branches and fillets, wreathes and masks in loose arrangement. With these products of the mere craftsman, which are often of fascinating effect (cp. Fig. 160), but often in shape and decoration cause one to miss the delicate taste of earlier times, ends the history of Greek vase-painting ; by pottery with relief ornament (already heralded by the completely black channelled vases of the 4th century and works like the aryballos of Xenophantos), which now gains ground more and more, painted pottery is completely driven off the field.

NOTE

Thanks are due to Messrs. F. Bruckmann, of Munich, for permission to reproduce several drawings from Furtwängler-Reichhold, *Griechische Vasenmalerei.*

INDEX OF ILLUSTRATIONS

Illustrations follow page 180.

PLATE I. Interior of a kylix signed by Euphronios as potter : from Caere; Paris, Louvre, G 104. Diameter O,39. From *Furtwängler-Reichhold* 5. *Frontispiece*

CHAPTER I. : THE STONE AND BRONZE AGES :—

Pl. II. Fig. 1. Bowl from Sesklo : Athens. Height O,20. Dark painting on lemon-coloured ground. From Tsountas, *Dimini and Sesklo* (Greek), pl. 22

Fig. 2. Face-urn from Troy II.-V. : Berlin. Height O,30. From *British School* yellowish clay. From *H. Schliemann's Sammlung Trojanischer Altertümer, Hubert Schmidt,* No. 1,080 and 1,084

Pl. III. Fig. 3. Beaked jug from Syros : Athens, Nicole 123. Height O,16. Light-brown painting on yellow ground. From *Ephemeris Arch.* 1899, pl. 10. No. 8

Fig. 4. Beaked jug from the sixth shaft-grave at Mycenae : Athens, Nicole 189. Height O,30. Turned on the wheel, polished, lustreless brown (and red) painting. From Furtwängler and Löschcke, *Mykenische Tongefässe,* pl. IX. No. 44.

Pl. IV. Fig. 5. Vase of Kamares style from the palace of Knossos : Candia. Height, O,22. Painting white, orange and carmine-red on black glaze. From *British School Annual* IX, p. 120.

Fig. 6. Unpainted kylix with y e l l o w smoothed surface, from the fourth shaft-grave at Mycenae : Athens, Nicole 164. Diameter O,12. From Furtwängler and Löschcke, *Mykenische Tongefässe,* pl. V. No. 22

Pl. V. Fig. 7. Funnel-vase of late Minoan I. from a house at Palaikastro : Candia. Height O,10. Turned on the wheel, *Annual* IX, p. 311, fig. 10

Fig. 8. Funnel-vase of late Minoan I. from house on the island of Pseira : Candia. From Seager, *Excavations on the island of Pseira,* p. 25, fig. 8

161

Fig. 9. Vase (Pithos) of Kamares style from Phaistos : Candia. Height O,50 Red and white painting on black glaze. From *Monumenti Antichi* XIV, pl. XXXV b

Pl. VI. Fig. 10. Stirrup-vase of late Minoan I., from a house at Gournia : Candia. Height O,20. From H. Boyd Hawes, *Gournia,* pl. H

Fig. 11. Amphora of late Minoan I., from a house on Pseira. With many details overpainted in white. From Seager *op. cit.,* pl. VII.

Pl. VII. Fig. 12. Amphora of Palace style from a grave of Knossos. From *Archæologia,* 1905, pl. CI

Fig. 13. Amphora of Palace style from a grave of Knossos. From *Archæologia,* 1905, pl. C.

Pl. VIII. Fig. 14. Late Mycenean Cup from Ialysos (Rhodes) : London. Height O,20. Dark-brown glaze-colour on yellow ground, details in white. From Furtwängler-Löschcke, *M y k e n i s-che Vasen,* pl. VIII, 49

Fig. 15. Late Mycenean stirrup-vase from Ialysos (Rhodes) : London. Height O,23. Yellowish-red glaze-colour on yellow ground. The tentacles of the cuttle-fish from a peculiar ornament on the reverse, a bird by the side of it. From Furtwängler-Löschcke, *Mykenische Vasen,* pl. IV., 24

Pl. IX. Fig. 16. Late Mycenean vase with ribbed handles from Ialysos (Rhodes) : London. Height O,34. Dark-brown glaze-colour (in parts burnt red) on yellow ground. From Furtwängler-Löschcke, *M y k e n i s c h e Vasen,* pl. VI., 32

Fig. 17. Late Mycenean vase with ribbed handles from Rhodes : Munich 47. Height O,45. Brown, partly red,

162

glaze-colour on yellow ground. Biga with driver and companion. *Münchener Vasensammlung* I., p. 6, fig. 7

CHAPTER II. : THE GEOMETRIC STYLE :—

Pl. X. Fig. 18. Attic Geometric Amphora (Dipylon class) : Munich 1,250. Height O,50. From photo.

Fig. 19. Geometric Amphora, said to come from Melos, probably Attic (Black Dipylon) : Munich. Height O,73. *Münchener Jahrbuch,* 1909, II., p. 202, fig. 1

Pl. XI. Fig. 20. Upper half of a Dipylon grave-vase : A t h e n s, Collignon-Couve 214. Height I,23. From *Monumenti dell' Istituto* IX., pl. 40, 1

Fig. 21. Frieze from the upper half of a bowl from Thebes, of which the rest is only decorated with stripes : London. From *Journal of Hellenic Studies,* 1899, pl. 8

Pl. XII. Fig. 22. Rhodian Geometric jug, said to come from Crete : Munich 455. Height O,22. *Münchener Vasensammlung* I., p. 44, fig. 57

Fig. 23. Protocorinthinian Geometric cup (skyphos) from Greece : Munich. Height O,12. *Münchener Jahrbuch,* 1913, I., p. 78

Pl. XIII. Fig. 24. Attic Geometric kylix from Athens : Munich. Diameter O,18. *Münchener Jahrbuch,* 1913, I., p. 78.

CHAPTER III. : THE SEVENTH CENTURY :—

Fig. 25. Cretan hydria from Praisos : Candia. Height O,30. From *British School Annual,* IX., pl. 9c

Fig. 26. Cretan jug from Praisos : Candia. Height O,33. White on glaze. From *B.S.A.* IX., pl. 9d

Pl. XIV. Fig. 27. Cretan miniature jug with female head : Berlin 307. Height O,10. From *Athenische Mitteilungen,* 1897, pl. 6

Fig. 28. Fragment of a jug from Aegina : Athens. Nicole 848. Diameter ca. O,25. *Athenische Mitteilungen,* 1897, pl. VIII.

Pl. XV. Fig. 29. Fragment of a plate from a grave at Praisos : Candia. Original diameter ca. O,35. Wrestle with a sea monster. From *B.S.A.* X., pl. III.

Fig. 30. Krater of Aristonothos : Rome, Palazzo dei Conservatori. Height O,36. From *Mélanges d' Archéologie et d' histoire,* 1911, pl. I.

Pl. XVI. Fig. 31. Protocorinthian lekythos : London, B.M. Height O,07. From *Journal of Hellenic Studies,* XI., pl. I., 2

Fig. 32. Protocorinthian lekythos, said to come from Corinth : Berlin 336. Height O,06. From *Archäologische Zeitung,* 1883, I.

Fig. 33. Protocorinthian jug of post-Geometric style from Aegina : Munich 225a. Height O'18. *Münchener Vasensammlung* I., p. 11, fig. 17

Pl. XVII. Fig. 34. Protocorinthian lekythos, said to come from Thebes : Boston. Height O,07. From *American Journal of Archæology,* 1900, pl. IV.

Pl. XVIII. Figs. 35-7. Protocorinthian jug, from the neighbourhood of Rome : Rome, Villa di Papa Giulio. Height O,26. From *Antike Denkmäler* II., pls. 44 and 45

Pl. XIX. Fig. 38. Protocorinthian or Corinthian jug : Munich 234. Height O,44. From photo.

Fig. 39. Corinthian alabastron, from Greece : Cambridge, Fitzwilliam Museum 30. Height O,20. From *Catalogue,* pl. IV.

Fig. 40. Corinthian aryballos, from Greece : Cambridge, Fitzwilliam Museum 36. Height O,20. From *Catalogue,* pl. IV.

Pl. XX. Fig. 41. Animal frieze from an early Corinthian jug : Munich 228. *Münch. Vasens.* I., p. 12, fig. 18

Fig. 42. Animal frieze from a Corinthian jug of wine-skin shape : Munich 246. *Münch. Vasens.* I., p. 16, fig. 24

Pl. XXI. Fig. 43. Corinthian skyphos, from Samos : Boston. Height O,08. From photo.

Fig. 44. Scene from the late Corinthian flask of Timonidas, from Kleonai (Peloponnese) : Athens, Collignon-Couve 620. Height of vase O,14. From *Athenische Mitteilungen,* 1905, pl. VIII.

Pl. XXII. Fig. 45. Pinax (votive-tablet), from Corinth, signed by Timonidas : Berlin 846. Height O,22. From *Antike Denkmäler* I., pl. 8, 13

Fig. 46. Frieze of an early Phaleron jug, from Analatos (Attica) : Athens, Collignon-Couve 468. From *Jahrbuch,* 1887, pl. 3

Pl. XXIII. Figs. 47-8. Neck and body designs of an early Attic Amphora, from Athens : A t h e n s, Collignon-Couve 657. Height I,22. From *Antike Denkmäler* I., pl. 57

Pl. XXIV. Fig. 49. Early Attic Amphora, from Piraeus : Athens, Collignon-Couve 651. Height I,10. From *Ephemeris,* 1897, pl. 5

Fig. 50. Cycladic (Euboic) Amphora : Stockholm. Height O,59. From *Jahrbuch,* 1897, pl. 7

Pl. XXV. Fig. 51. Jug with griffin's head, from Aegina : London, B.M., A 547. From photo.

Pl. XXVI. Fig. 52. Chief design on a " Melian " amphora, from Melos : Athens, Collignon-Couve 475. Height of amphora O,95. From Conze, *Melische Tongefässe,* pl. IV.

Pl. XXVII. Fig. 53. Herakles and Iole (?) on a "Melian" amphora, said to come from Crete : Athens, Collignon-Couve 477. From *Ephemeris,* 1894, pl. 13

Fig. 54. Early Rhodian jug, from Rhodes : H a g u e, Scheurleer Collection. Height O,22. From photo.

165

Pl. XXVIII. Fig. 55. Rhodian jug : Munich 449. Height O,33. *Münch Vasens.* I, p. 42, fig. 54

Fig. 56. Late Rhodian jug, from Rhodes : Munich 450. Height O,33. *Münch Jahrb,* 1911, II, p. 200

Fig. 57. Euphorbos plate, from Rhodes : London, B.M. Diameter O,38. From Photo

Pl. XXIX. Fig. 58. Late Rhodian cauldron (lebes), from Italy : Paris, Louvre. Height O,35. From photo.

Pl. XXX. Fig. 59. Gorgon plate, from Rhodes : London, B.M. From *J.H.S.,* 1885, pl. 59.

Fig. 60. Sherd from Naukratis : Oxford. (Busiris' head painted red on white slip, details by leaving the parts un-painted). From *J.H.S.,* 1905, pl. VI., I.

Fig. 61. Naukratite sherd found on the Acropolis of Athens : Athens, Acro-polis 450a. Yellow, red and white painting on bright ground. From *Akropolisvasen* I., pl. 24

Pl. XXXI. Fig. 62. Amphora, from Rhodes (Fikellura) : London, B.M., A 1311. Height O,34. From *Münchener Archäol : Studien,* p. 300, fig. 24.

Fig. 63. Amphora (Fikellura) : Altenburg. Height O,31. From Böhlau, *Nek-ropolen,* p. 56

CHAPTER IV. : THE BLACK-FIGURED STYLE :—

Pl. XXXII. Fig. 64. Two friezes of a Corinthian krater, from Caere : Paris, Louvre E. 635. Height O,46. After photo.

Fig. 65. Corinthian krater, from Corinth : Munich 344. Height O,31. *Münch Jahrb,* 1911, II., p. 290, fig. 1.

Pl. XXXIII. Fig. 66. Frieze of a Corinthian krater, from Caere : Berlin 1655. Height O,46. From *Monumenti* X, pl. 4, 5

Pl. XXXIV. Fig. 67. Corinthian plate : Munich 346a. Diameter O,28. *Münch Vasens.* I., p. 31, fig. 46

Fig. 68. Chalkidian hydria, from Italy: Munich 596. Height O,46. From photo.

Pl. XXXV. Fig. 69. Chalkidian amphora,, from Vulci: Würzburg. Height O,41. From photo.

Pl. XXXVI. Fig. 70. Chalkidian amphora, from Caere: London, B.M., B 155. Height O,45. From photo.

Fig. 71. Scene from Chalkidian amphora of Italian provenance: Munich 592. *Münch. Vasens.* I., p. 65, fig. 75

Pl. XXXVII. Fig. 72. Ionic eye kylix, from Italy: Munich 589. Height O,10. From photo.

Fig. 73. Head of Athena, from Ionic eye kylix: Munich 590. *Münch. Vasens.* I., p. 64, fig. 74.

Pl. XXXVIII. Fig. 74. Phineus kylix, from Vulci: Würzburg. Diameter O,39. From *Furtwängler-Reichhold* 41

Pl. XXXIX. Fig. 75. Ionic b.f. fragments, from Kyme (Asia Minor): London, B.M. From photo.

Fig. 76. Neck design of an Ionic b.f. Amphora, from Italy: Munich 586. *Münch. Vasens.* I., p. 62, fig. 73

Pls. XL.-I, Figs. 77-8. Obverse and reverse of an Ionic b.-f. Amphora, from Italy: Munich 585. From *Münch. Vasens.* I., p. 59, figs. 69 and 70.

Pl. XLII. Fig. 79. Chief design on a Caeretan hydria: Vienna, Museum für Kunst und Industrie 217. From *Furtwängler-Reichhold* 51

Fig. 80. Spartan kylix, from Italy: Munich 382. Height O,15. From *Münch. Vasens.* I., p. 34, fig& 48

Pl. XLIII. Fig. 81. Caeretan hydria, from Caere: Paris, Louvre E 701. Height O,43. From photo.

XLIV. Figs. 82-3. Obverse and reverse of a Pontic amphora, from Italy: Munich 837. Height of vase O,33. From *Furtwängler-Reichhold* 21

167

Pl. XLV. Fig. 84. Spartan kylix, from Corneto : Berlin. From *Jahrbuch d. D. Instatus* 1901, *pl. III.*

Pl. XLVI. Fig. 85. Spartan kylix (Arkesilas), from Vulci : Paris, Cabinet des Médailles 189. Diameter O,29. From *Monumenti* I., pl. 47A

Pl. XLVII. Fig. 86. Fragments of a cauldron (lebes) by Sophilos : Athens, Acropolis. Gräf 587. Height of the frieze O,09. From Gräf, *Akropolisvasen,* pl. 26

Fig. 87. Attic tripod vase, from Athens : Munich. Height O,12. From *Münch. Jahrb,* 1911, II., p. 291, fig. 5.

Pl. XLVIII. Fig. 88. Boeotian b.-f. kantharos : Munich 419. Height O,19. From *Münch. Vasens.* I., p. 40, fig. 52

Fig. 89. Detail of the François vase. From *Furtwängler-Reichhold,* 13

Pl. XLIX. Fig. 90. François vase, from Chiusi : Florence, Museo archeologico. Height O,66. From *Furtwängler-Reichhold,* pl. 3, 10

Pl. L. Fig. 91. ' Little Master ' kylix, from Vulci : Munich, Jahn 36. Height O,15. From photo.

Fig. 92. Attic b.-f. kylix with knob handles : Boston. From photo.

Pl. LI. Fig. 93. Interior of an eye kylix of Exekias, from Vulci : Munich, Jahn 339. Diameter O,30. From Gerhard, *Auserlesene Vasenbilder* I., pl. 49

Pl. LII. Fig. 94. Scene from an Attic b.-f. Amphora, from Vulci : Berlin 1685. Height of vase O'49. From Gerhard, *Etruskische und Kampanische Vasenbilder,* pl. 21

Pl. LIII. Fig. 95. Scene from an Attic b.-f. Amphora, probably from Vulci : Würzburg, Urlichs 331. From photo.

Pl. LIV. Fig. 96. Amphora of Exekias, from Vulci : Rome, Museo Gregoriano, Helbig 1220. Height of vase O,80. From photo.

GREEK VASE-PAINTING

Fig. 97. Attic b.-f. necked Amphora, from Italy : Munich. Height O,40. From photo.

Pl. LV. Fig. 98. Necked Amphora of Amasis : Paris Cabinet des Médailles 222. Height O,33. From photo.

Fig. 99. Detail from interior of a cauldron of Exekias, from Caere : formerly Castellani Collection, Rome. From *Wiener Vorlegeblätter,* 1888, pl. 5, 3 b

Pl. LVI. Fig. 100. Chief scene on a late b.-f. hydria, from Vulci : Berlin, 1897. Height of vase O,44. From Gerhard, *Auserlesene Vasenbilder* IV., pl. 249-50

Pl. LVII. Fig. 101. Attic vase in shape of negro's head with late b.-f. decoration of neck : Boston. From photo.

Fig. 102. Panathenaic Amphora, from Vulci : Munich, Jahn 655. Height O,62. From photo.

CHAPTER V. : THE RED-FIGURED STYLE IN THE ARCHAIC PERIOD :—

Pl. LVIII. Fig. 103. Scene on an Amphora in the style of the Andokides painter, from Vulci : Munich, Jahn 388. Height O,535. From *Furtwängler-Reichhold* 4

Pl. LIX. Fig. 104. Amphora of the potter Pamphaios (Nikosthenes' shape), from Etruria : Paris, Louvre G 2. Height O,38. From photo.

Pl. LX. Fig. 105. Scene on an Amphora of Euthymides, from Vulci : Munich, Jahn 378. Height O,60. From *Furtwängler-Reichhold* 14.

Fig. 106. Shoulder scene on a hydria of Hypsis, from Vulci : Rome, Torlonia Collection. From *Antike Denkmäler* II., pl. 8

Pl. LXI. Fig. 107. Detail of Amphora of Euthymides, from Vulci : Munich, Jahn 410. From photo.

Fig. 108. Detail from interior of an archaic r.-f. kylix, from Orvieto : Boston. From photo.

169

Pl. LXII. Fig. 109.   Rhyton (in shape of a horse's head) with r.-f. decoration of neck: Boston. From photo.

Pl. LXIII. Fig. 110.   Interior of a kylix by Skythes, from Caere: Rome, Villa di Papa Giulio. Diameter of interior O,10. From *Monuments Piot XX.*, pl. 7

Pl. LXIV. Fig. 111.   Interior of a kylix by Epiktetos, from Vulci. London, B.M., E. 38. From *Furtwängler-Reichhold* 73, 1

Pl. LXV. Fig. 112.   Part of the design on the psykter of Euphronios, from Caere. Petrograd, Hermitage, 1670. From *Furtwängler-Reichhold* 63

Pl. LXVI. Fig. 113.   Obverse of a kalyx-krater of Euphronios, from Caere. Paris, Louvre G 103. Height of krater O,46. From *Furtwängler-Reichhold* 92

Pl. LXVII. Fig. 114.   Kylix signed by the potter Sosias, from Vulci: Berlin 2278. Diameter O'32. From photo.

Pl. LXVIII. Fig. 115.   Interior of a r.-f. kylix, from Caere: formerly Branteghem Collection, now London, B.M., E 46. From Hartwig, *Griechische Meisterschalen*, pl. VIII.

Pl. LXIX. Fig. 116.   Interior of a kylix of Brygos, from Vulci: Würzburg, Urlichs (1872) 346. From photo.

Pl. LXX. Fig. 117.   Detail of an archaic r.-f. pointed amphora, from Vulci: Munich, Jahn 408. From Photo.

Pl. LXXI. Figs. 118-9.   Exteriors of a kylix of Brygos: Paris, Louvre. From *Furtwängler-Reichhold* 25

Pl. LXXII. Fig. 120.   R.-f. skyphos, from Italy: Vienna, Museum für Kunst und Industrie 328. From photo.

Fig. 121.   Exterior of a kylix, from Corneto: Corneto. From *Monumenti XI.*, pl. 20

Pl. LXXIII. Fig. 122.   Scene on a psykter of Duris, from Caere: London, B.M., E. 768. Height of vase O,29. From *Furtwängler-Reichhold* 48

Pl. LXXIV. Fig. 123.   Kylix of Hieron, from Vulci: Berlin 2290. Diameter O,33. From photo.

Pl. LXXV. Fig. 124. Kylix of Duris, from Caere : Berlin 2285. Diameter O,28. From photo.

Fig. 125. R.-f. kylix, from Vulci : Berlin 2294. Diameter O,30. From photo.

Pl. LXXVI. Fig. 126. Interior of a r.-f. kylix, from Vulci : Munich, Jahn 368. Diameter O,305. From *Furtwängler-Reichhold* 86.

CHAPTER VI. :
THE STYLE OF POLYGNOTOS AND PHEIDIAS.

Pl. LXXVII. Fig. 127. Figure on a skyphos of Pistoxenos, from Caere : Schwerin. From *Jahrbuch des D. Instituts* 1912, pl. 6

Fig. 128. Detail of a fragmentary white-ground lekythos, from Attica : Bonn. From *J.H.S.* 1896, pl. 4

Pl. LXXVIII. Fig. 129. Kylix with white-ground interior, from Rhodes : London, B.M. D 2. Diameter O,24. From photo.

Fig. 130. Detail of a r.-f. krater : New York. From photo.

Pl. LXXIX. Fig. 131. Obverse of a r.-f. krater, from Sicily (?) : Boston. Height of vase O,36. From *Furtwängler-Reichhold* 115, 1

Pl. LXXX. Fig. 132. Fragmentary r.-f. psykter, from Falerii : Rome, Villa di Papa Giulio. From photo.

Fig. 133. Interior of a kylix, of the potter Hegesibulos : Brussels : *Münch. Jahrb.* 1913, II., p. 89

Pl. LXXXI. Fig. 134. Interior of a r.-f. kylix, from Etruria : Munich, Jahn 370. Diameter O,425. From *Furtwängler-Reichhold* 6

Pl. LXXXII. Fig. 135. Obverse of a r.-f. kylix-krater, from Orvieto : Paris, Louvre G 341. Height of vase O,55. From *Furtwängler-Reichhold* 108

Pl. LXXXIII. Figs. 136-7. Design on lid and sides of a pyxis of Megakles : Bibliothèque Royale, Brussels. Height O,063. Diameter O,085. From Fröhner, *Coll. Barre*, pl. VII.

171

Fig. 138. Detail of a r.-f. pointed amphora : Paris, Cabinet des Médailles 357. From *Furtwängler-Reichhold,* pl. 77,[1]

Pl. LXXXIV. Fig. 139. Scene on a r.-f. pelike, from Rugge (Apulia) : Lecce. From *Furtwängler-Reichhold* 66

Fig. 140. Scene on a r.-f. krater, from Gela : Berlin. Height of vase O,50. From *50 Berliner Winckelmannsprogramm* (1890)

Pl. LXXXV. Fig. 141. R.-f. Amphora, from Vulci : London, B.M., E 271. Height O,57. From photo.

Pl. LXXXVI. Fig. 142. White-ground lekythos, from Attica : London, D 58. Height ca. O,48. From photo.

Pl. LXXXVII. Figs. 143-4. Youth and maiden on a white-ground lekythos, from Attica : Boston 8440. Height of vase, O,40. From photo.

Fig. 145. Detail of a white-ground lekythos : Athens, Collignon-Couve 1822. From Furtwängler-Riezler, *Weissgrundige Lekythen,* pl. 93

Pl. LXXXVIII. Fig. 146. R.-f. stamnos, from Vulci : Munich, Jahn 382. Height O,445. From photo.

Fig. 147. Scene on a r.-f. stamnos, from Campania : Naples, Heydemann 2419. From photo.

Pl. LXXXIX. Fig. 148. Scene on a r.-f. Amphora, from neighbourhood of Arezzo : Arezzo. Height of vase O,54. From *Furtwängler-Reichhold,* pl. 67

Pl. XC. Figs. 149-51. Three details of a fragmentary r.-f. vase : Naples. From three photos. in the Munich Vase Collection

Pl. XCI. Fig. 152. Scene on a r.-f. hydria, from Populonia : Florence. Height of vase O,46. From Milani, *Monumenti scelti,* pl. 4

Pl. XCII. Fig. 153. R.-f. volute amphora, from Ruvo : Ruvo, Jatta Collection 1501. Height of frieze O,35. From *Furtwängler-Reichhold* 38.

Pl. XCIII. Fig. 154. Scene on a r.-f. jug : Oxford. Height of vase O,21. From *J.H.S.* 1905, pl. 1.

CHAPTER VII. : LATE OFFSHOOTS :—

Fig. 155. Scene on a late Attic pelike, from Kerch (Crimea) : Petrograd, Hermitage 1795. Height O,38. From *Furtwängler-Reichhold* 87,2.

To face page

Pl. XCIV. Fig. 156. Lucanian bell-krater, from the Basilicata : Paris, Louvre. Height O,53. From photo.

Fig. 157. Lower Italian bell-krater with comedy scene (Phlyax vase), from Apulia. London, B.M., F. 151. Height of vase O,39. From photo.

Pl. XCV. Fig. 158. Apulian volute amphora, from Bari : Boston. Height I,25. From photo.

Pl. XCVI. Fig. 159. Late Attic kalyx-krater, from Greece : Munich. Height O,41. From *Münch. Jahrb,* 1913, I., p. 79

Fig. 160. Hellenistic cup with designs painted in white : Munich. Height O,09. From *Münch. Jahrb,* 1909, II. p. 204, fig. 8

173

INDEX OF NAMES

The names of painters and potters are printed in italics. All are Athenian, unless it is otherwise stated.

ACHAEANS, 16.
Achilles, 46, 65, 68, 125, 128, 129, 139, 157.
Acropolis (of Athens), 99, 103, 110, 114, 115, 122, 137, 153.
Acropolis sculptures, 50.
Adonis, 152.
Ægean Sea, 17.
Ægina, 6, 14, 26, 32, 42, 49, 50, 52, 53, 60.
Æolians, 17.
Æolis, 90.
Africa, 89, 92.
Aias, 68, 79, 156.
Aison, 151.
Aktaion, 137.
Alabastron, 44.
Alexandria, 110, 159.
Alkmaion, 73.
Altenburg, amphora at, 61, 84.
Amasis, 97, 102, 103, 105, 106, 107, 108, 113, 116, 127, 136, 143.
Amazons, 75, 81, 84, 139, 141.
Amphiaraos, 67, 71, 72, 73, 143, 144.
Amphitrite, 126.
Amphora, 24, 49, 52, 54, etc.; (big-bellied), 50, 74, 104; (necked), 51, 74; (pointed), 126, 127; (Nolan), 127, 136; (with twisted handles), 149; (Panathenaic), 99, 110, 127, 153.
Anakreon, 114, 135.
Andokides, 58, 108, 109, 114, 115, 117, 118, 120, 121.
' *Andokides* ' *painter,* 115, 131.
Antaios, 123, 124, 125, 126.
Antenor (sculptor), 112, 131.
Aphidna (Attica), 6.
Aphrodite, Temple of, 42.
Aphrodite, 135, 137, 152.
Apollo, 25, 54, 55, 65, 139.
Apulia, 156.

Apulian vases, 157.
Arezzo, amphora at, 149.
Argive alphabet, 59.
Argolid, The, 5, 6, 7, 12, 19, 26, 33, 42.
Argonaut Master, The, 140-2.
Argonauts, The, 140, 147.
Argos (giant), 86.
Argos (town), 14, 26, 33.
Ariadne, 22, 129.
Aristagoras (kalos), 130.
Aristonothos (? Aristonoos, perhaps Argive), 33, 38.
Aristophanes, 151.
Arkesilas, king, 92.
Artemis, 55, 137.
Artemis the Persian, 54.
Aryballos, 44, 142, 158.
Asia Minor, 5, 6, 15, 17, 19, 42, 55, 80, 87, 191.
Assarlik, 19.
Assteas (Campanian painter), 156.
Astyanax, 65.
Athena, 49, 65, 66, 67, 68, 71, 81, 99, 100, 106, 110, 126, 147, 153.
Athenodotos (kalos), 126.
Athens, 19, 51, 96, 99, 106, 111, 121, 157.
Athens, Vases in, 139, 147, 149.
Attica, 6, 25, 42, 51.

BARBOTINE, 8.
Beaked jug, 5.
Bellerophon, 39, 40, 64.
Berlin amphora, Master of the, 131.
Berlin, Vases in, 92, 104, 109, 130, 131, 133, 134, 135, 139.
Black Sea, 28, 56, 89, 158.
Boeotia (Boeotians), 2, 22, 26, 42, 52, 60, 94, 96, 110, 155.
Bonn, Vases in, 119, 134, 135.
Boreas, 82.

174

INDEX OF NAMES

Boreas, Sons of, 82.
Boston, Vases in, 45, 100, 126, 130, 135, 137, 146. 147, 157.
Bowl (Schüssel), 22, 66.
Bronze Age, 2, 3, 4.
Bronze-foundry Master, 131.
Brygos painter, 128, 129, 131, 139.
Bucchero ware, 90.
Busiris (Pharaoh), 89.
Butades (Sicyonian), 69.

CABLE PATTERN (Guilloche), 30, 35.
Caere, 42, 68.
Caeretan hydriae, 87-9, 107.
Campania, 156.
Carthage, 42.
Castle Ashby, Amphora at, 86, 87.
Centaurs, 22, 39, 86, 89, 98, 128, 140, 150.
Centauromachy, 91, 130.
Chairestratos (kalos), 126, 127, 129.
Chalkidian style, 69, 70, 75-80, 94, 96, 97, 100, 104, 105, 106, 107, 118.
Chalkis, 71, 75, 76, 77, 80, 94, 96, 99, 100, 105, 106, 108.
Chares (Corinthian painter), 45.
Charitaios, 101, 103.
Chelis, 121.
Chigi jug, 38, 40, 45, 59, 66.
Chimaera, The, 39, 40.
Circe, 100, 146.
Corfu, 44.
Corinth, 26, 34, 42, 50, 56, 69, 70, 90, 94, 100.
Corinthian style, 43, 50, 70-75, 90, 94, 96.
Corneto, Vases in, 123, 129.
Cretans, 10, 12, 34.
Crete, 1, 2, 13, 14, 15, 16, 17, 19, 27, 33, 55.
Cyclades, 15, 25, 94.
Cycladic (pottery, etc.), 5, 6, 25, 52, 54, 80.

Cyprus, 5, 6, 14, 15, 17, 26.
Cyrene, 92.

'DAEDALIC' TYPES, 34.
Daedalus, 31.
Daphne, 86.
Deianeira, 34.
Deiniades, 119, 123.
Delian (or Euboic) ware, 53, 81.
Delos, 25, 54, 55, 98.
Delphi, 26.
Delta, The, 56, 59.
Demeter, 135.
Dimini, 2.
Diomede, 79.
Dionysos, 66, 82, 96, 97, 100, 106, 108, 148, 149.
Dipylon (Athens), 1, 24, 27, 35.
Dörpfeld (Wilhelm), 4.
Dorians, The, 17, 19.
Duris, 120, 126, 129, 130, 131, 139.

EGYPT, 9, 15, 83.
Egyptian, 89.
Eleusis, 6, 25, 26.
Eos, 130, 135.
Ephesian sculpture, 88.
Epiktetos, 108, 114, 121, 122, 123, 124.
Epilykos (kalos), 120-3.
Eretria, 25, 52, 94.
Eretria master, The, 148, 152, 153.
Erginos, 151.
Ergoteles, 101.
Ergotimos, 97, 100, 101, 103.
Eriphyle, 73, 143, 144.
Ethos, 133, 142.
Etruria, 90, 91, 94, 99, 156.
Etruscan, 1, 35, 90.
Euboea, 25, 52.
Euboic (or Delian) ware, 53.
Eucheiros, 101.
Eumares, 111, 112.
Euphorbos plate, 58.
Euphrates, The, 12.

175

Euphronios, 18, 109, 114, 116, 117, 120, 122-9, 131, 133, 134, 135, 139.
Europa, 68, 88.
Eurytios, 72, 79, 97.
Euthymides, 114, 116-9, 122, 123, 125, 127.
Euxitheos, 117, 123.
Exekias, 68, 101, 102, 103, 105, 107, 108, 113, 115.

FACE URNS, 4.
  ' Fates,' The, 152.
Fibulae, 22.
Fikellura (Samian) ware, 60-2, 83, 116.
Flamed ware, 7.
Florence, Vase in, 97.
François vase, 71, 95, 96, 97-9, 100, 101, 103, 104, 108.
Funnel vase, 12.
Furtwängler, Adolf, 20, 64.

GALES, 114.
  Ge, 139.
Gela, 143, 144.
Geometric style, 16, 17, 18, 19, 20, 22-8, 29, 31, 41, 54, 56, 69, 135, 144.
Geryon, 78, 79.
Gigantomachia, 150.
Glaukon, son of Leagros (kalos), 114, 124, 130, 133, 134, 135, 137, 138, 145.
Gnathia vases, 157.
Gorgon, 44, 50, 58, 101.
Gorgon lebes, 49, 66, 97, 100.
Griffin head jug, 53.

HADRA VASES, 110.
  Halimedes, 73.
Hamilton, Sir William, 1.
Harpies, 50, 82.
Head, Vases in shape of, 120, 142 (Figs. 101, 109).
Hector, 59, 118, 129.
Hegesibulos, 142.
Helen, 22, 23, 118.

Helios, 150.
Hellenistic painting, 159.
Hephaistos, 66, 67, 71, 88, 98.
Herakles, 39, 50, 54, 60, 64, 65, 66, 67, 71, 72, 75, 79, 89, 99, 115, 116, 123, 124, 126.
Hermes, 40, 49, 86, 88, 145.
Hermogenes (kalos), 130.
Hermonax, 143.
Heröon, 157.
Hesiod, 22.
Hetairai, 116, 119, 120, 123, 146.
Hieron, 131, 135.
Hipparchos (kalos), 109, 114.
Hippodamas (kalos), 127, 130.
Hippodameia, 149.
Hischylos, 101, 121, 122.
Hissarlik (Troy), 4.
Homer, 16, 22.
Homeric poems, 17, 71, 135 (see *Iliad* and *Odyssey*).
Horse master, 128, 133, 137, 138, 139.
Hydria, 67, 74, 108, 109, 119.
Hygieia, 152.
Hymettos, 48.
Hymn (Homeric), 55.
Hypsis, 119, 125.

IDA, Mt., 8.
  Iliad, The, 59, 65, 125, 147.
Iliupersis, 67, 104, 128.
Io, 86.
Iole, 72, 73.
Ionia, 47, 94.
Ionians, 17, 62.
Ionic art, 25, 55-62, 79-89, 120.
Isocephalism, Law of, 68.
Italy, 15, 26, 42, 60, 90.

JAPANESE ART, 12.
  Jug with rotelle, 41-3, 57; wine- skin-shaped, 41.

KABIRION, 110.
  Kachrylion, 123.
Kalistanthe (kale), 102.

INDEX OF NAMES

Kalliades, 130.
Kallinos, 92.
Kaloi, 102, 114.
Kamares style, 5, 8, 9, 10, 11, 13.
Kantharos, 96, 120, 129.
Kassandra, 156.
Kavusi, 27, 30.
Kerameikos, 121.
Kerch style, 158.
Kimon (statesman), 134.
Kimon of Kleonai, 111.
Klazomenai, 83, 84, 87, 116.
Klazomenian sarcophagi, 87, 111.
Klazomenian style, 83, 84.
Kleanthes (Corinthian painter), 65, 67.
  Kleophrades' painter, 127.
Kleophrades, son of Amasis, 127. 129.
Klitias, 18, 97, 98, 101, 103, 104, 108, 113.
Klytemnestra, 156.
Knossos, 10, 14.
Kolchos, 87, 103, 104, 107.
Korone, 118.
Krater, 15, 33, 34, 71, 72, 73, (a colonnette) 74, ,(calyx) 123, 136, 140, 142, (bell) 127, 136, 149, 156, (volute) 157.
Kyknos, 78.
Kylix (bird), 26, 52, 94, (eye) 81, (with offset rim) 91.
Kyme (Italy), 27, 28, 42, 53.
Kypselos, Chest of, 67, 71, 78, 95.

L ANUVIAN JUNO, 90.
  Leagros, father of Glaukon (kalos) ,109, 114, 115, 120, 121, 123, 124, 125, 126, 127, 130, 134, 142.
Lebes (cauldron) 49, (bronze) 53, 57, 66, 71, (with stand) 74, 86, 91, 95, 108.
Lecce, Pelike at, 143.
Leto, 55.
Leukas, 5, 6.
Lion Gate, The, 7.

Little Masters, 101, 102, 105.
London, Vases in, 58, 61, 78, 108, 119, 122, 125, 126, 130, 135, 143, 145, 147, 149, 156.
Lotus, 11.
Loutrophoros in Athens, 134.
Louvre (see Paris).
Lower Italy, Vases of, 153, 155, 158.
Lucania, 156.
Lydos (the Lydian), 103.

M ADRID, VASES IN, 116, 151.
Maenads, 66, 100, 106, 127, 131, 143.
Makron, 131, 135.
Marathon, 114, 115, 140.
Marina (Hagia), 5, 6.
Massilia, 28.
Mattmalerei (lustreless painting), 6.
Medusa, 49, 50.
Megakles (Alkmaeonid), 114, 119.
Megakles (potter), 142, 152.
Meidias, 18, 149, 151, 157.
Meleager, 98.
' Melian ' vases, 53-5, 81.
Melos, 5, 9, 12, 14, 25, 53.
Melusa, 145.
Memnon (epic hero), 65.
Memnon (kalos), 114, 121, 123.
Menelaos, 104.
Menon, painter, 116.
Metallic effect in vase shapes, 76.
Metope maeander, 57, 61.
Metopes, 21.
Miletus, 25, 30, 55, 56, 114.
Minoan style (1), Early, 5, 7,; (2), Middle, 8, 9; (3), Late, 10, 12, 13, 14.
Minos, 7.
Minotaur, 66, 104.
Minyan ware, 6.
Mnasalkes (Theban), 52.
Mochlos (Crete), 7.
Monochromy, 33, 44, 48.

Munich, Vases in, 76, 78, 86, 96, 102, 107, 115, 117, 118, 123, 127, 128, 130, 135, 138, 139, 145, 148.

Musaios, 145.

Muse, 95, 145.

Mycenae, 6, 7, 12, 14.

Mycenean, 1, 7, 8, 13, 14—19 (late).

NAPLES, 1.
Naples, Vases in, 148, 150, 153.

Naturalistic style, 11, 13.

Naukratis, 43, 51, 58, 59, 60, 61, 83, 88, 91, 101.

Nauplia, 19.

Nearchos, 101, 103, 104, 112.

Neolithic, 2, 5.

Neoptolemos, 104.

Nereids, 89.

Nessos vase, 47, 48, 49, 50, 51.

New York, Vase in, 134, 142.

Nike balustrade, 151.

Nikosthenes, 87, 101, 103, 108, 115, 116, 121, 122.

Nile, The, 9, 12.

Nolan style, 131.

Nudity, 20.

Nymph, 82, 150.

ODYSSEUS, 79, 100.
Odyssey, 32.

Oichalia, 72.

Oltos, 116, 119, 122, 123, 124, 127.

Olympia, 15, 53, 67.

Olympos, 65, 66, 67, 71.

Onesimos (?), 128.

Onetorides (kalos), 106.

Orchomenos (Boeotia), 5, 6, 14.

Orestes, 156.

Oriental art, 29-32, 35, 37.

Orpheus, 137, 139.

Orvieto, Calyx-Krater from, 140.

Oxford, Vases in, 114, 150.

PAIDIA, 152.
Palace style (second late Minoan), 13, 14.

Palaisto, 124.

Pamphaios, 101, 103, 108, 109, 115, 116, 121, 122, 123.

' Pan ' Master, The, 137.

Panaitios (kalos), 126, 127.

' *Panaitios* ' Master, The, Frontispiece, 126, 128, 129, 130.

Panathenaea, The, 99.

Panathenaic amphorae (see *Amphora*).

Paris (of Troy), 22, 40, 152.

Paris, Vases in : (1) Louvre, 49, 58, 72, 79, 91, 94, 105, 108, 116, 123, 126, 128, 130, 140, 156; (2) Cabinet des Médailles, 92, 106, 143.

Parthenon, 144, 147, 148, 150, 151.

Patroklos, 125.

Pausanias (Descriptio Graeciæ), 71.

Pedieus (kalos), 109.

Pegasus, 39.

Peithinos, 124.

Peleus, 32, 33, 71, 95.

Pelias, 67.

Pelike, 110, 119, 143.

Peloponnese, 17, 90.

Pelops, 149, 150, 155.

Penthesileia, 81, 138.

Penthesileia Master, The, 139, 141.

Periclean age, 144.

Perseus, 49, 59, 64.

Perugia Master, The, 128, 130, 139.

Petrograd, Psykter in, 123.

Phaistos, 10, 14.

Phaleron style, 47, 48, 49, 54.

Phaon, 152.

Pheidias, 113, 142, 143, 144, 148, 151, 154.

' Phineus ' style, 80-3, 102, 105, 107, 121.

INDEX OF NAMES

Phineus kylix, 76, 79, 80, 81, 93, 146, 150.
Phintias, 114, 119, 123, 125.
Phlyakes, 156.
Phocis, 2, 5.
Phœnicia, 15.
Phœnician metal work, 30, 47, 55, 58.
Physiognomy, 135, 139.
Pinax (votive tablet), 46, 51, 114.
Piraeus amphora, 49.
Pisistratidae, 114.
Pisistratus, 99.
Pistoxenos, 122, 134.
Plate (Teller), 32, 58.
Pliny, 111, 112.
Polychromy, 8, 10, 60, 93 (see *Kamares, Naukratis.*)
Polygnotan vases, 140, 141.
Polygnotos, 123, 133, 138, 143, 146.
Polygnotos (vase painter), 143.
Polyneikes, 144.
Polyphemus, 33.
' Pontic ' vases, 89, 90.
Pontus, 43.
Poseidon, 65, 126.
Praisos, 31, 32, 36, 46, 59.
Praxiteles, 158.
Priam, 104, 117, 123.
' *Pronomos* ' *Master, The,* 151, 153, 154.
Protocorinthian, 26, 27, 34, 36, 37, 38, 41, 42, 43, 44, 47, 49, 53, 56, 59, 71, 75, 120.
Psiax, 121.
Psykter, 119, 120, 123, 130, 137, 140.
Pylos, 14.
Pyros (Theban), 52.
Python, 122, 129.

RAM JUG, 32, 53.
Rankengeschling, 36.
Rays, Circle of, 35.
Red-figured style, 87, 102, 109, 111-3.

Rheneia, 25, 54.
Rhodes, 1, 15, 17, 26, 30, 42, 61, 135.
Rhodian ware, 56-9, 81.
Rome, Vases in, 105, 122.
Rotelle, 41, 57.
Russia, South, 83, 158.

SAMOS (see Fikellura), 30, 43, 61, 91.
Sarcophagi (see Klazomenai).
Sarpedon, 65, 147.
Satyrs, 45, 66, 75, 79, 82, 84, 88, 92, 96, 98, 100, 107, 116, 119, 120, 126, 130, 150.
Schliemann, Heinrich, 4, 7.
Schwerin, Vase in, 134.
Scythians, 75, 81, 84, 89.
Selene, 150.
Sesklo, 2.
Shaft graves (Mycenæ), 6, 7, 12.
Sicily, 15, 26, 42, 60.
Sicyon, 34 (see *Butades*).
Sicyonian-Corinthian metal work, 41.
Silenus, 81.
Silhouette, 31, 32, 37.
Silphion, 92.
Sirens, 45, 95.
Skopas, 158.
Skyphos (two-handled cup), 35, 38, 45, 120, 128, 134.
Skythes (the Scythian), 121, 122, 123.
Sleep and Death, 145, 147.
Smikros, 120.
Sophilos, 71, 95, 96, 97, 99, 104.
Sosias kylix, 79, 124, 125.
' *Sosias* ' *painter,* 125, 127.
Sotades, 120, 142, 153.
Sparta, 26, 47, 90.
Spartan ware, 90-3, 122.
Spata, 14.
Sphinx, 39, 40, 45.
Stamnos, 119, 136, 143, 145, 148.
Stesagoras (kalos), 114.

179

Stesias (kalos), 105.
Stesichoros, 99.
Sthenelos, 79.
Stirrup-vase, 12, 19.
Stockholm, Vase in, 52.
Stone Age, 1, 2, 3, 7.
Stylized ornament, 11.
Syracuse, 28, 34, 42.

TALEIDES, 104.
Talos vase, 154, 155, 157.
Tectonic style, 11, 13 .
Terpsichore, 145, 149.
Textile influence, 23.
Thamyris, 152.
Thera, 9, 12, 25, 26, 27, 42, 53, 111.
Thebes, 14, 22.
Thersites, 157.
Theseus, 22, 66, 98, 118, 126, 129, 130, 151.
Thessaly, 2, 3, 5, 6.
Thetis, 32, 65, 71, 95, 97.
Thorikos (Attica), 14.
Thracian women, 137.
Timagoras, 67, 108.
Timonidas (Corinthian), 45, 46, 51, 72, 113.
Tintoretto, 158.
Tiresias, 156.
Tiryns, 5, 33.
Titian, 158.
Tityos, 139.
Tleson, 101.
Tragodia, 151.
Triada Hagia (Crete), 14.
Tripod vase, 96.
Triptolemos, 135.
Triton, 67, 89, 108.

Troilos, 45, 65, 81, 91, 98, 108.
Troy, 4, 5, 6, 17, 129.
Turin, Psykter in, 119.
' Tyrrhenian' vases, 99, 100, 103, 106.
Tyrtaios, 92.

VAPHIO, 14.
Vase shapes (see Alabastron, Amphora, Aryballos, Beaked jug, Bowl, Face urn, Funnel-vase, Head, Hydria, Jug, Kantharos, Krater, Kylix, Lebes, Loutrophoros, Pelike, Plate, Psykter, Sky-phos, Stamnos, Stirrup vase, Tripod vase).
Veii, 42.
Vienna, Vases in, 119, 128, 129.
Villa Giulia Master, The, 143.
Volo, 14.
Vurvá vases, 47, 50, 51, 83, 93, 95, 100.

WALL PAINTING (see Butades, Eumares, Kimon of Kleonai, Kleanthes, Poly-gnotos), 16, 31, 33, 67, 68, 138, 158.
Warrior vase (from Mycenae), 15, 33.
Würzburg, Vases in (82), 105, 106, 128.

XENOPHANTOS, THE ATHENIAN, 158.

ZEUS, 65, 147.

Plates

Fig. 1.   STONE AGE BOWL FROM THESSALY.

Fig. 2.   FACE-URN FROM TROY II—V.

PLATE II.

Fig. 3. JUG FROM SYROS.

Fig. 4. JUG FROM MYCENÆ.

PLATE III.

Fig. 5. KAMARES VASE FROM KNOSSOS.

Fig. 6. KYLIX FROM MYCENÆ

PLATE IV.

Figs. 7 & 8. FUNNEL-VASES OF LATE MINOAN I STYLE.
FROM PALAIKASTRO AND PSEIRA.

Fig. 9. KAMARES PITHOS FROM PHAISTOS.

PLATE V.

Fig. 10. STIRRUP-VASE OF LATE MINOAN I STYLE FROM GOURNIA.

Fig. 11. AMPHORA OF LATE MINOAN I STYLE FROM PSEIRA.

PLATE VI.

Figs 12 & 13. AMPHORÆ OF THE PALACE STYLE FROM KNOSSOS.

PLATE VII.

Fig. 14. LATE MYCENEAN CUP FROM RHODES.

Fig. 15. LATE MYCENEAN STIRRUP-VASE FROM RHODES.

PLATE VIII.

Figs. 16 & 17.   LATE MYCENEAN VASES FROM RHODES.

PLATE IX.

Fig 18. ATTIC GEOMETRIC AMPHORA (DIPYLON CLASS)

Fig. 19.
GEOMETRIC AMPHORA,   PROBABLY ATTIC (BLACK DIPYLON CLASS).

PLATE X.

Fig. 20.   UPPER HALF OF A DIPYLON GRAVE-VASE.

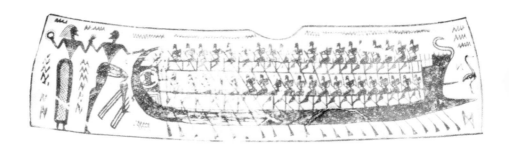

Fig. 21.   'THE RAPE OF HELEN,' ON A BOWL FROM THEBES.

PLATE XI.

Fig. 22. RHODIAN GEOMETRIC JUG.

Fig 23. PROTOCORINTHIAN GEOMETRIC SKYPHOS.

PLATE XII.

Fig. 24.   ATTIC GEOMETRIC KYLIX.

Figs. 25 & 26.   CRETAN JUGS IN THE FIRST ORIENTALISED STYLE.

PLATE XIII.

Fig. 27. CRETAN MINIATURE JUG.

Fig. 28. THE FLIGHT FROM THE CAVE OF POLYPHEMUS,
FROM A JUG FROM ÆGINA.

PLATE XIV.

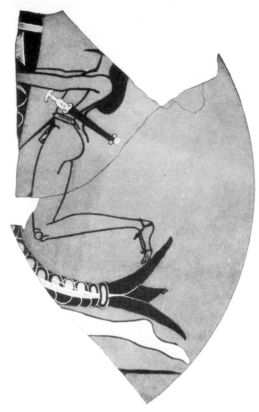

Fig. 29.   HERAKLES AND SEA-MONSTER (?) FROM A CRETAN PLATE.

Fig. 30.   ARGIVE KRATER WITH THE SIGNATURE OF ARISTONOTHOS :
SEVENTH CENTURY.
PLATE XV.

Fig. 31.

Fig. 32.

PROTOCORINTHIAN LEKYTHOI WITH BATTLE-SCENE AND
SLAUGHTER OF THE CENTAURS.

Fig. 33.

PROTOCORINTHIAN JUG OF POST-GEOMETRIC STYLE FROM ÆGINA
EARLY SEVENTH CENTURY.

PLATE XVI.

Fig. 34. BELLEROPHON AND THE CHIMAERA FROM A PROTO-
CORINTHIAN LEKYTHOS.

Fig. 35. PROTOCORINTHIAN JUG, KNOWN AS THE CHIGI VASE.

PLATE XVII.

Figs. 36 & 37. SCENES FROM THE CHIGI JUG: HARE AND LION HUNT; CHARIOT.

PLATE XVIII.

Fig. 38. PROTOCORINTHIAN OR CORINTHIAN JUG.

Fig. 39.   Fig. 40.

CORINTHIAN ALABASTRON AND ARYBALLOS.

PLATE XIX

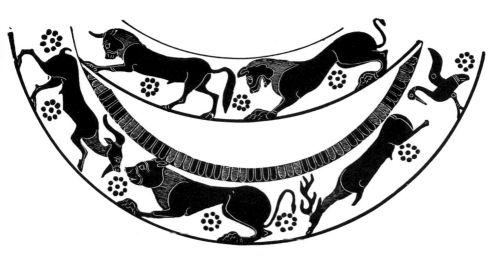

Fig. 41   ANIMAL FRIEZE FROM AN EARLY CORINTHIAN JUG.

Fig 42.   ANIMAL FRIEZE FROM A CORINTHIAN JUG.

PLATE XX.

Fig. 43. CORINTHIAN SKYPHOS

Fig. 44. ACHILLES AND TROILOS : FROM THE LATE CORINTHIAN
FLASK BY TIMONIDAS.

PLATE XXI.

Fig. 45. HUNTER AND HOUND. PINAX FROM CORINTH,
SIGNED BY TIMONIDAS.

Fig. 46. FRIEZE OF AN EARLY PHALERON JUG.

PLATE XXII.

Figs. 47 & 48. HERAKLES AND THE CENTAUR NESSOS ; THE GORGONS :
NECK AND BODY DESIGNS OF AN ATTIC AMPHORA.

PLATE XXIII.

Fig. 49. ATTIC AMPHORA.

Fig. 50. CYCLADIC (EUBOIC) AMPHORA.

PLATE XXIV.

Fig. 51. CYCLADIC JUG WITH GRIFFIN'S HEAD FROM ÆGINA.

PLATE XXV.

Fig. 52. ARTEMIS, APOLLO, ARGE AND OPIS: FROM A "MELIAN" AMPHORA.

PLATE XXVI.

Fig. 53   HERAKLES AND IOLE (?): FROM A 'MELIAN' AMPHORA.

Fig. 54.   EARLY RHODIAN JUG.

PLATE XXVII.

Fig. 55. RHODIAN JUG.

Fig. 56. LATE RHODIAN JUG.

Fig. 57. EUPHORBOS PLATE FROM RHODES : MENELAOS AND
HECTOR FIGHTING OVER THE BODY OF EUPHORBOS.

PLATE XXVIII.

Fig. 58. LATE RHODIAN CAULDRON (LEBES).

PLATE XXIX.

Fig. 59. GORGON PLATE FROM RHODES.

Fig. 60 & 61. BUSIRIS; HERAKLES: NAUKRATITE SHERDS FROM
NAUKRATIS AND ATHENS.

PLATE XXX.

Figs. 62 & 63. FIKELLURA AMPHORÆ.

PLATE XXXI.

Fig 64. HERAKLES AND EURYTIOS; HORSEMEN: FROM A
CORINTHIAN KRATER.

Fig. 65. CORINTHIAN KRATER.

PLATE XXXII.

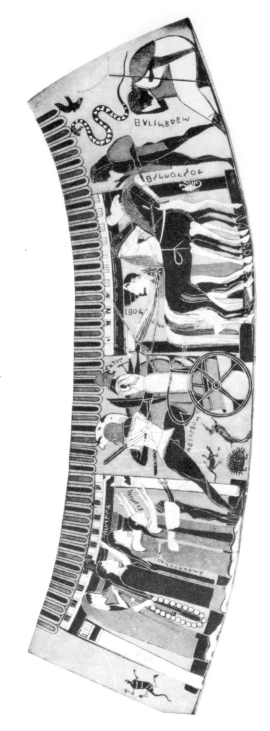

Fig. 66. DEPARTURE OF AMPHIARAOS : FROM A CORINTHIAN KRATER.

PLATE XXXIII.

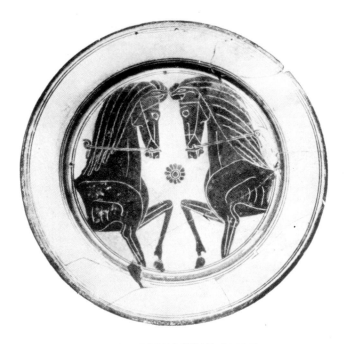

Fig. 67. CORINTHIAN PLATE.

Fig.68. THE SLAYING OF TYPHON BY ZEUS : CHALKIDIAN HYDRIA

PLATE XXXIV.

Fig. 69. CHALKIDIAN AMPHORA.

PLATE XXXV.

Fig. 70.
HERAKLES AND GERYONEUS: FROM A CHALKIDIAN AMPHORA.

Fig. 71. THE SLAYING OF KYKNOS BY HERAKLES: FROM A
CHALKIDIAN AMPHORA.

PLATE XXXVI.

Fig. 72. IONIC EYE KYLIX.

Fig. 73.
HEAD OF ATHENA, BETWEEN THE EYES OF AN IONIC EYE KYLIX

PLATE XXXVII.

Fig. 74.

PHINEUS; DIONYSOS: FRIEZE ROUND THE INTERIOR OF AN IONIC
EYE KYLIX.

From Furtwängler-Reichhold, Griechische Vasenmalerei.

PLATE XXXVIII.

Fig. 75. SATYR AND MAENAD: KLAZOMENIAN VASE FROM KYME

Fig. 76. NECK-DESIGN OF AN IONIC AMPHORA.

PLATE XXXIX.

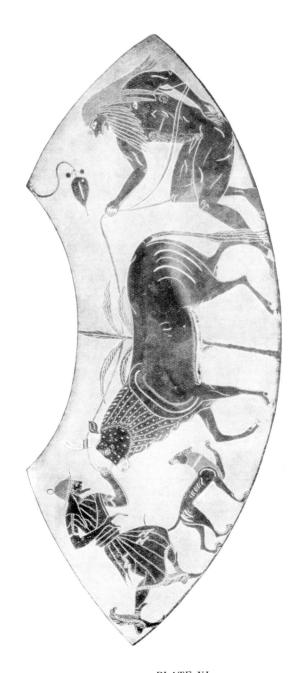

Fig. 77. HERMES STEALS THE COW IO FROM THE GIANT ARGOS : FROM AN IONIC AMPHORA.

PLATE XL.

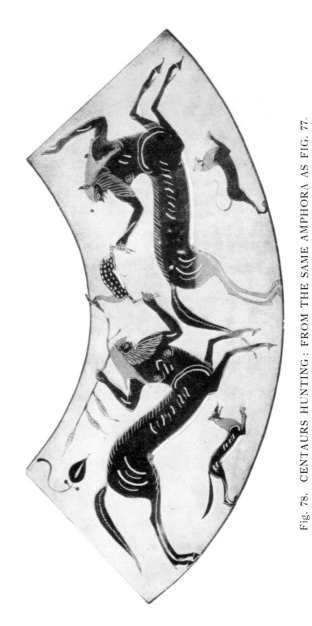

Fig. 78. CENTAURS HUNTING: FROM THE SAME AMPHORA AS FIG. 77.

PLATE XLI.

Fig. 79. HERAKLES SLAYS BUSIRIS AND HIS FOLLOWERS: FROM A
CÆRETAN HYDRIA.

From Furtwängler-Reichhold, Griechische Vasenmalerei.

Fig. 80. SPARTAN KYLIX.

PLATE XLII.

Fig. 81. HERAKLES BRINGS CERBERUS TO EURYSTHEUS:
CÆRETAN HYDRIA.

PLATE XLIII.

Figs. 82 & 83. PARIS AND HIS HERD; PRIAM AND HERMES LEAD HERA,
ATHENA AND APHRODITE BEFORE PARIS: FROM A PONTIC AMPHORA.

From Furtwängler-Reichhold, Griechische Vasenmalerei.

PLATE XLIV.

Fig. 84. RETURNING FROM BATTLE: FROM A SPARTAN KYLIX

PLATE XLV.

Fig. 85   ARKESILAS OF CYRENE WATCHING THE LADING OF
SILPHION : FROM A SPARTAN KYLIX.

PLATE XLVI.

Fig. 86. WEDDING OF PELEUS: FRAGMENTS OF A CAULDRON BY
SOPHILOS.

Fig. 87. ATTIC TRIPOD-VASE.
PLATE XLVII.

Fig. 88.   BŒOTIAN KANTHAROS.

Fig. 89.   ARRIVAL OF THESEUS' SHIP AT DELOS : DETAIL OF THE
FRANÇOIS VASE, FIG. 90.

From Furtwängler-Reichhold, Griechische Vasenmalerei.

PLATE XLVIII.

Fig. 90.

KRATER BY KLITIAS AND ERGOTIMOS: "THE FRANCOIS VASE."

From Furtwängler-Reichhold, Griechische Vasenmalerei.

PLATE XLIX.

Fig. 91.   'LITTLE MASTER' KYLIX.

Fig. 92.   ATTIC KYLIX WITH KNOB-HANDLES.

PLATE L.

Fig. 93. DIONYSOS: INTERIOR OF AN EYE KYLIX BY EXEKIAS.

PLATE LI.

Fig. 94. ILIUPERSIS: FROM AN ATTIC AMPHORA.

PLATE LII.

FIG. 95. SATYRS AT THE WINE-PRESS: FROM AN ATTIC AMPHORA.

PLATE LIII.

Fig. 96. ACHILLES AND AIAS PLAYING AT DRAUGHTS: FROM AN
AMPHORA BY EXEKIAS.

Fig. 97. ATTIC NECKED AMPHORA WITH SATYR-MASK.

PLATE LIV.

Fig. 98.
NECKED AMPHORA WITH THE SIGNATURE OF THE POTTER AMASIS.

Fig. 99.   DETAIL FROM THE INTERIOR OF A CAULDRON BY EXEKIAS.

PLATE LV.

Fig. 100. FROM A LATE ATTIC BLACK-FIGURED HYDRIA.

PLATE LVI.

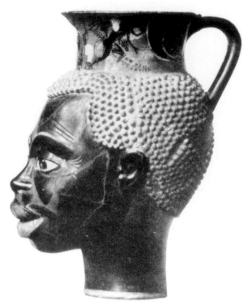

Fig. 101. ATTIC VASE, LATE BLACK-FIGURED STYLE.

Fig. 102. PANATHENAIC AMPHORA
PLATE LVII.

Fig. 103. ATHENA AND HERAKLES: FROM AN AMPHORA IN THE STYLE OF THE ANDOKIDES PAINTER.

From Furtwängler-Reichhold, Griechische Vasenmalerei.

PLATE LVIII.

Fig. 104. HETAIRA ; SATYR AND MAENAD : AMPHORA WITH THE
SIGNATURE OF THE POTTER PAMPHAIOS.

PLATE LIX.

Fig. 105.

THE ARMING OF HECTOR: FROM AN AMPHORA BY EUTHYMIDES.

From Furtwängler-Reichhold, Griechische Vasenmalerei.

Fig. 106. FOUNTAIN: FROM A RED-FIGURED HYDRIA BY HYPSIS.

PLATE LX.

Fig 107.   THE RAPE OF KORONE BY THESEUS: FROM AN AMPHORA
BY EUTHYMIDES.

Fig. 108.   DRUNKEN SATYR: FROM AN ARCHAIC RED-FIGURED KYLIX.
PLATE LXI.

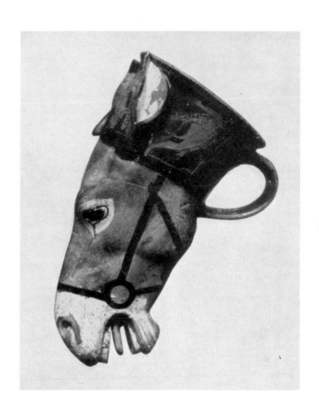

Fig. 109. RHYTON WITH RED-FIGURED DECORATION ON THE NECK.

PLATE LXII.

Fig. 110.   DRUNKEN LYRE-PLAYER : FROM A KYLIX BY SKYTHES.

PLATE LXIII.

Fig. 111. FLUTE-PLAYER AND DANCING GIRL: FROM A KYLIX BY
EPIKTETOS.

From Furtwängler-Reichhold, Griechische Vasenmalerei.

PLATE LXIV.

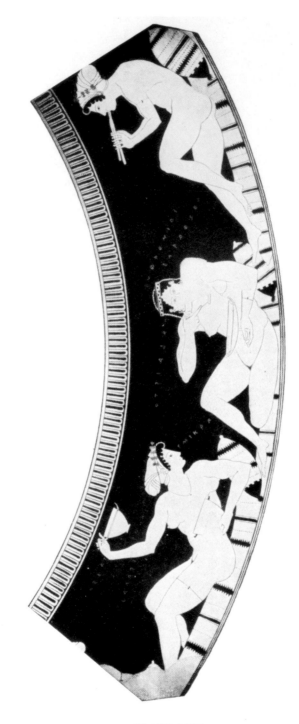

Fig. 112. HETAIRAI: FROM A PSYKTER BY EUPHRONIOS.

From Furtwängler-Reichhold, Griechische Vasenmalerei.

PLATE LXV.

Fig. 113. HERAKLES AND ANTAIOS: FROM A KALYX-KRATER BY EUPHRONIOS.

From Furtwängler-Reichhold, Griechische Vasenmalerei.

PLATE LXVI.

Fig. 114. ACHILLES AND PATROKLOS: FROM A KYLIX WITH THE
SIGNATURE OF THE POTTER SOSIAS.

PLATE LXVII.

Fig. 115. BOY CHASING A HARE: RED-FIGURED KYLIX.

PLATE LXVIII.

Fig. 116. AFTER THE BANQUET: FROM A KYLIX WITH THE
SIGNATURE OF THE POTTER BRYGOS.

PLATE LXIX.

Fig. 117. A MAENAD IN FRENZY: FROM AN ARCHAIC
RED-FIGURED POINTED AMPHORA.

PLATE LXX.

Figs. 118 & 119. THE SACK OF TROY: FROM A KYLIX WITH THE SIGNATURE OF THE POTTER BRYGOS.

From Furtwängler-Reichhold, Griechische Vasenmalerei.

PLATE LXXI.

Fig. 120. SKYPHOS WITH THE RANSOMING OF HECTOR.

Fig. 121. THESEUS DESERTS THE SLEEPING ARIADNE (?): FROM THE
EXTERIOR OF A KYLIX.

PLATE LXXII.

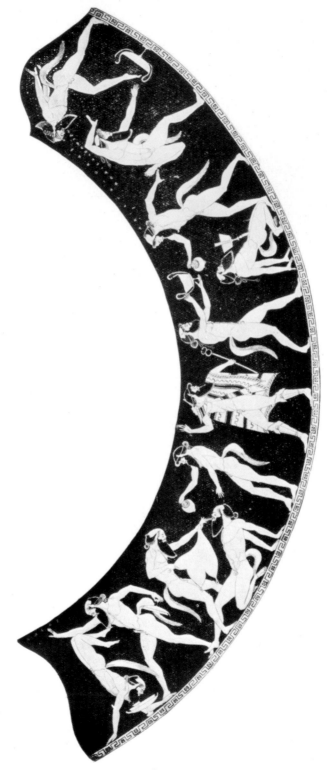

Fig. 122. HERMES AND SATYRS: FROM A PSYKTER BY DURIS.

From Furtwängler-Reichhold, Griechische Vasenmalerei.

PLATE LXXIII.

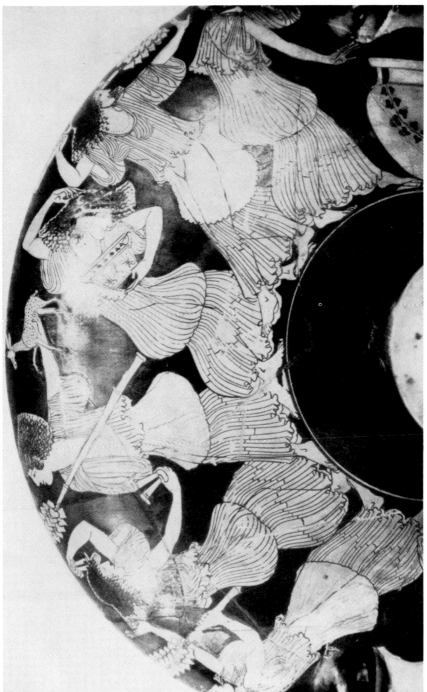

Fig. 123. DRUNKEN MAENADS: FROM A KYLIX WITH THE SIGNATURE OF THE POTTER HIERON.

PLATE LXXIV.

Fig. 124. SCHOOL-SCENE : FROM A KYLIX BY DURIS.

Fig. 125. BRONZE-FOUNDRY : FROM A KYLIX WITH THE " LOVE-
NAME " OF DIOGENES.

PLATE LXXV.

Fig. 126. CENTAUROMACHY : FROM A RED FIGURED KYLIX.

PLATE LXXVI.

Fig. 127.   OLD WOMAN : FROM A SKYPHOS WITH
THE SIGNATURE OF THE POTTER PISTOXENOS.

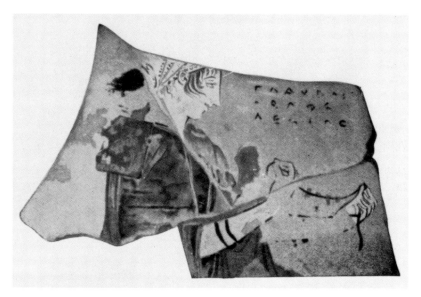

Fig. 128.   DETAIL OF A FRAGMENTARY WHITE-GROUND LEKYTHOS

PLATE LXXVII.

Fig. 129. APHRODITE ON A GOOSE: FROM A KYLIX WITH WHITE-GROUND INTERIOR, BEARING THE "LOVE-NAME" OF GLAUKON.

Fig. 130. WARRIOR: FROM A RED-FIGURED KRATER.

PLATE LXXVIII.

Fig. 131. THE DEATH OF AKTAION : FROM A RED-FIGURED KRATER.

From Furtwängler-Reichhold, Griechische Vasenmalerei.

PLATE LXXIX.

Fig. 132. BATTLE WITH CENTAURS: RED-FIGURED PSYKTER.

Fig. 133.
TOP-PLAYER: FROM A WHITE-GROUND KYLIX WITH THE
SIGNATURE OF THE POTTER HEGESIBULOS.

PLATE LXXX.

Fig. 134. ACHILLES KILLS PENTHESILEIA : INTERIOR OF A RED-
FIGURED KYLIX.

From Furtwängler-Reichhold, Griechische Vasenmalerei.

PLATE LXXXI.

Fig 135.   THE ARGONAUTS (?).   KALIX-KRATER OF POLYGNOTAN PERIOD.

From Furtwängler-Reichhold, Griechische Vasenmalerei.

PLATE LXXXII.

Figs. 136 & 137.

LID AND SIDE OF A PYXIS WITH THE SIGNATURE OF THE POTTER
MEGAKLES.

Fig. 138.   MAENADS : FROM A RED-FIGURED POINTED AMPHORA.

PLATE LXXXIII.

Fig. 139. POLYNEIKES OFFERS ERIPHYLE THE NECKLACE: FROM A
RED-FIGURED PELIKE.

From Furtwängler-Reichhold, Griechische Vasenmalerei.

Fig. 140.
ORPHEUS AMONG THE THRACIANS: FROM A RED-FIGURED KRATER.

PLATE LXXXIV.

Fig. 141. MUSIC: RED FIGURED NECKED AMPHORA.

PLATE LXXXV.

Fig. 142. SLEEP AND DEATH CARRY OUT A WARRIOR TO BURIAL:
WHITE-GROUND LEKYTHOS.

PLATE LXXXVI.

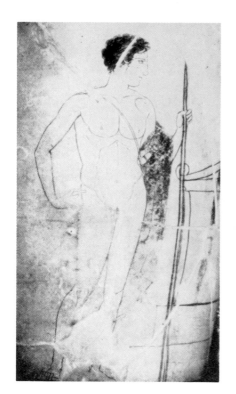

Figs. 143 & 144.   YOUTH AND MAIDEN ON A WHITE-GROUND LEKYTHOS

Fig. 145.   WOMAN SEATED AT A GRAVESTONE: FROM A WHITE-
GROUND LEKYTHOS.

PLATE LXXXVII.

Fig. 146. RED-FIGURED STAMNOS.

Fig. 147. OFFERINGS AT THE IMAGE OF DIONYSOS: FROM A RED-FIGURED STAMNOS.

PLATE LXXXVIII.

Fig. 148. PELOPS AND HIPPODAMEIA: FROM A RED-FIGURED NECKED AMPHORA.

From Furtwängler-Reichhold, Griechische Vasenmalerei.

PLATE LXXXIX.

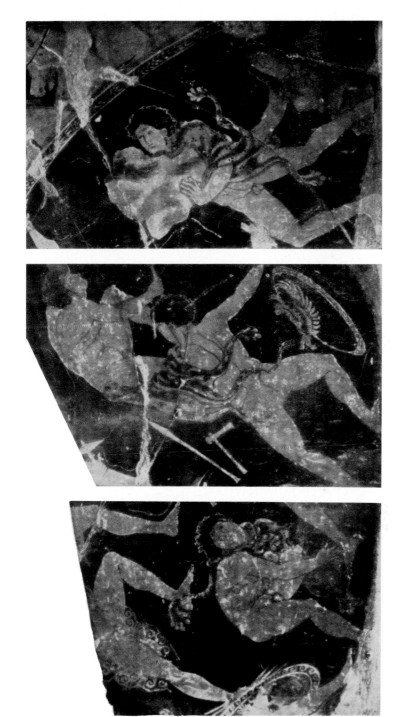

Figs. 149—151. GIGANTOMACHIA: FRAGMENT OF A RED-FIGURED KRATER.

PLATE XC.

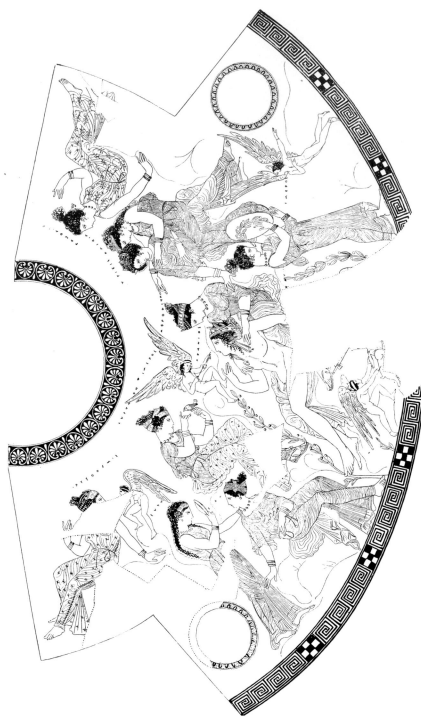

Fig. 152. ADONIS AND APHRODITE: FROM A RED-FIGURED HYDRIA

PLATE XCI.

Fig. 153. THE GIANT TALOS OVERCOME BY THE DIOSKUROI : RED-FIGURED VOLUTE-KRATER.

PLATE XCII.

Fig. 154.   SATYR AND SLEEPING MAENAD : FROM A RED-FIGURED JUG.

Fig. 155.   WOMEN AT THE BATH : FROM A LATE ATTIC PELIKE.

From Furtwängler-Reichhold, Griechische Vasenmalerei.

PLATE XCIII.

Fig. 156. ORESTES AND THE FURIES: FROM A LUCANIAN BELL-KRATER

Fig. 157. COMEDY SCENE: LOWER-ITALIAN BELL-KRATER.

PLATE XCIV.

Fig. 158. ACHILLES AND THERSITES: APULIAN VOLUTE-KRATER.
PLATE XCV.

Fig. 159. LATE ATTIC KALYX-KRATER.

Fig. 160. HELLENISTIC CUP.

PLATE XCVI.